The Resources of Papua New Guinea

SOCIAL SCIENCE PUPIL BOOK

Department of Education
Papua New Guinea

First Published 1988
Reprinted 1990, 1993, 1994, 1995, 1996 (twice), 1997, 1998, 1999 (twice), 2000 (twice), 2002, 2008, 2014(D)

ISBN 9980 58210 3

National Library of Papua New Guinea

Designed by Steve Randles
Illustrated by Chris Johnston and Cas Bukor
Typeset by Abb Typesetting Pty Ltd, Collingwood, Victoria, Australia
Printed in Australia by Ligare Pty Ltd
Published by Department of Education, Papua New Guinea
Prepared by Oxford University Press
253 Normanby Road, South Melbourne, Australia

Acknowledgements

This book was written by Brian Deutrom, Mike McRory and Andy Vicars of the Curriculum Unit, Port Moresby, and Anne and Michael Crossley. The Papua New Guinea Department of Education acknowledges the contribution of many individuals at the Curriculum Unit and on the Social Science Syllabus Advisory Committee to the review of this book. The textbook development was co-ordinated by Mike McRory, Senior Curriculum Officer for Social Science at the Curriculum Unit.

The authors and publishers wish to thank copyright holders for supplying, and granting permission to reproduce, the following photographs and maps:

Associated Press, courtesy of the *Herald*, p. 25 (lower right);

Robert Brown & Associates, Sydney (adaptation from D. King and S. Ranck (eds), *Papua New Guinea Atlas: A Nation in Transition*, 2nd edn), p. 28;

Bougainville Copper Limited, p. 46;

Dale Mann, Retrospect, p. 58;

National Archives of Papua New Guinea, pp. 4, 7, 15 (lower right), 18 (lower right), 19 (top left), 26 (lower right), 27 (upper and lower right), 29 (upper and lower right), 37 (upper and lower), 44, 53;

Ok Tedi Mining Limited, pp. 43, 45;

Pacific Expeditions, p. 30;

Papua New Guinea Institute of Applied Social and Economic Research, Plate I (C. F. Pain), p. 16; Plate II (G. S. Humphreys), p. 17, Plate VII (J. Powell), p. 38, in L. Morauta, J. Pernetta and W. Heaney (eds), *Traditional Conservation in Papua New Guinea: Implications for Today*, IASER Monograph 16, 1982.

Secretary's Message

The topic **The Resources of Papua New Guinea** is the second term's work in the Grade Eight Provincial High School Social Science Course. It is the second of four topics which explore the theme **People and Environment** through Grades Seven to Ten.

The book is the core learning material for the topic. A supporting set of teaching notes is available. The teaching notes advise the teachers on how to make the best use of the pupil's book and other resources for this topic.

The material in this book integrates the presentation of information, the development of ideas, the reinforcement and application of Social Science skills and the fostering of positive attitudes.

Three types of activities appear at the end of each section. There are *Exercises* to ensure comprehension of the material and to develop skills; there are *Things to discuss* and *Things to do*. The activities combine work on sections of the book with direct investigations both inside and outside the school.

J. E. Tetaga
Secretary for Education

This book is one of the items of instructional material produced for Provincial High Schools in Papua New Guinea as part of the Education III Text book Sub-Project.

Contents

1. What Is a Resource?

Introduction

A resource is anything we use. For example, *kaukau* is a food resource for many Papua New Guineans; the milk from pawpaw leaves is a traditional medicinal resource for cleaning wounds; and a *kwila* tree is a resource if we want to make a canoe or build a house. These are all **natural resources**; that means we can find them in nature.

However, we sometimes need human knowledge and skill to make a resource useful. Kaukau is not a food resource until we realize it is edible. Pawpaw leaves are a medicinal resource only for people who know how to use them. They are not a resource for people who do not have this knowledge. In the same way, a kwila tree only becomes a resource when we have the **technology** to turn it into a canoe or timber for a house. People with such skills and knowledge are **human resources**.

Here are two examples of how people use technology to make natural resources useful. This process is called manufacturing.

Manufacturing

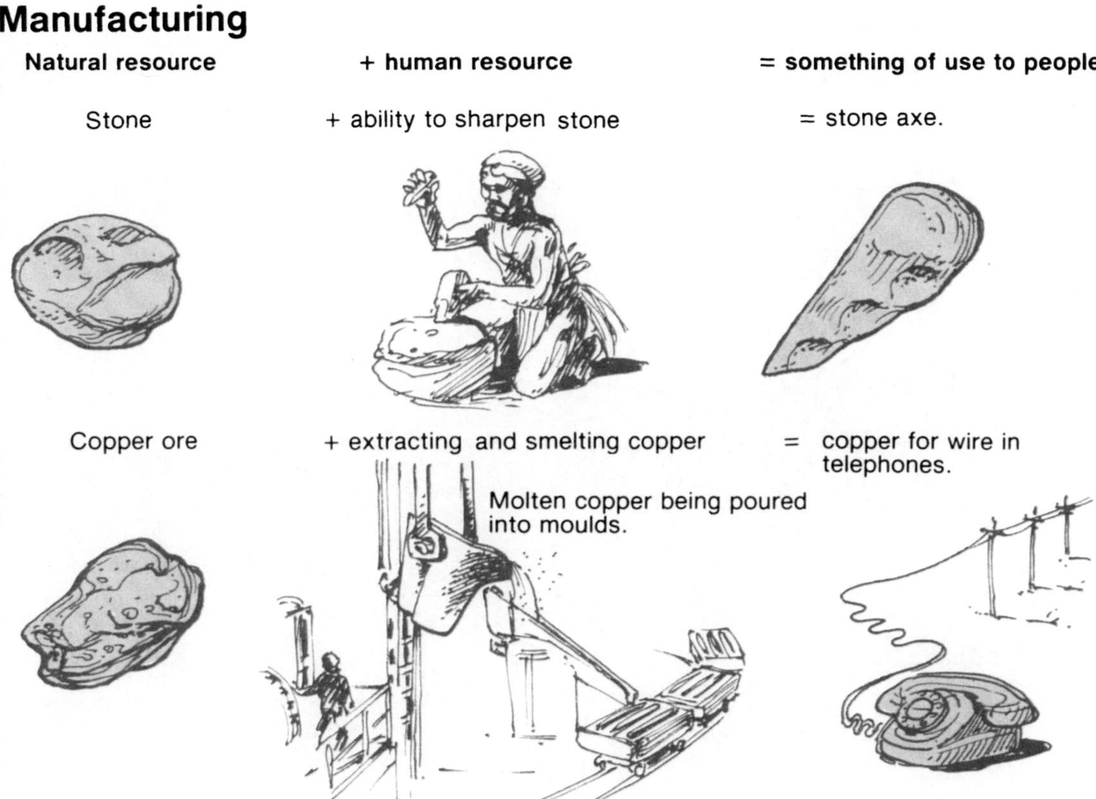

Renewable and Non-renewable Resources

Some resources are never likely to run out. Such a resource is the air we breathe. Some resources are renewable. This means we can replace them. For example, if we plant and look after a tree for each one we cut down, the world will always have trees. Many people have realized this in the past. On the south coast of Manus, for example, people planted *kwila* trees in order to provide wood for their grandchildren's canoes. In this way the clan ensured that it always had tall straight trees for canoes.

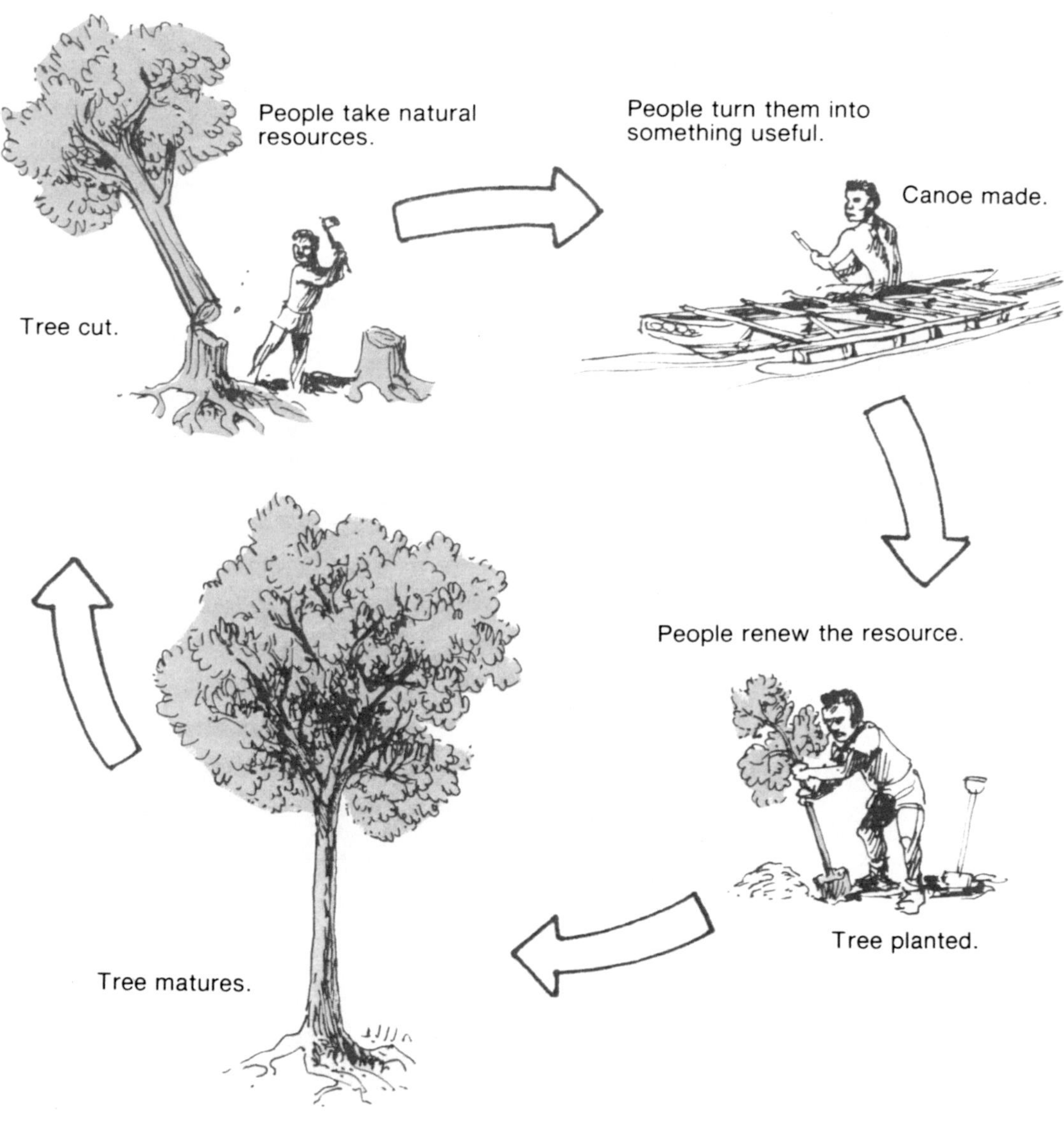

Some resources are **non-renewable**. Mineral oil and copper are examples of such resources. When we use these resources nature does not replace them. They are gone for ever. This is shown in the following diagram.

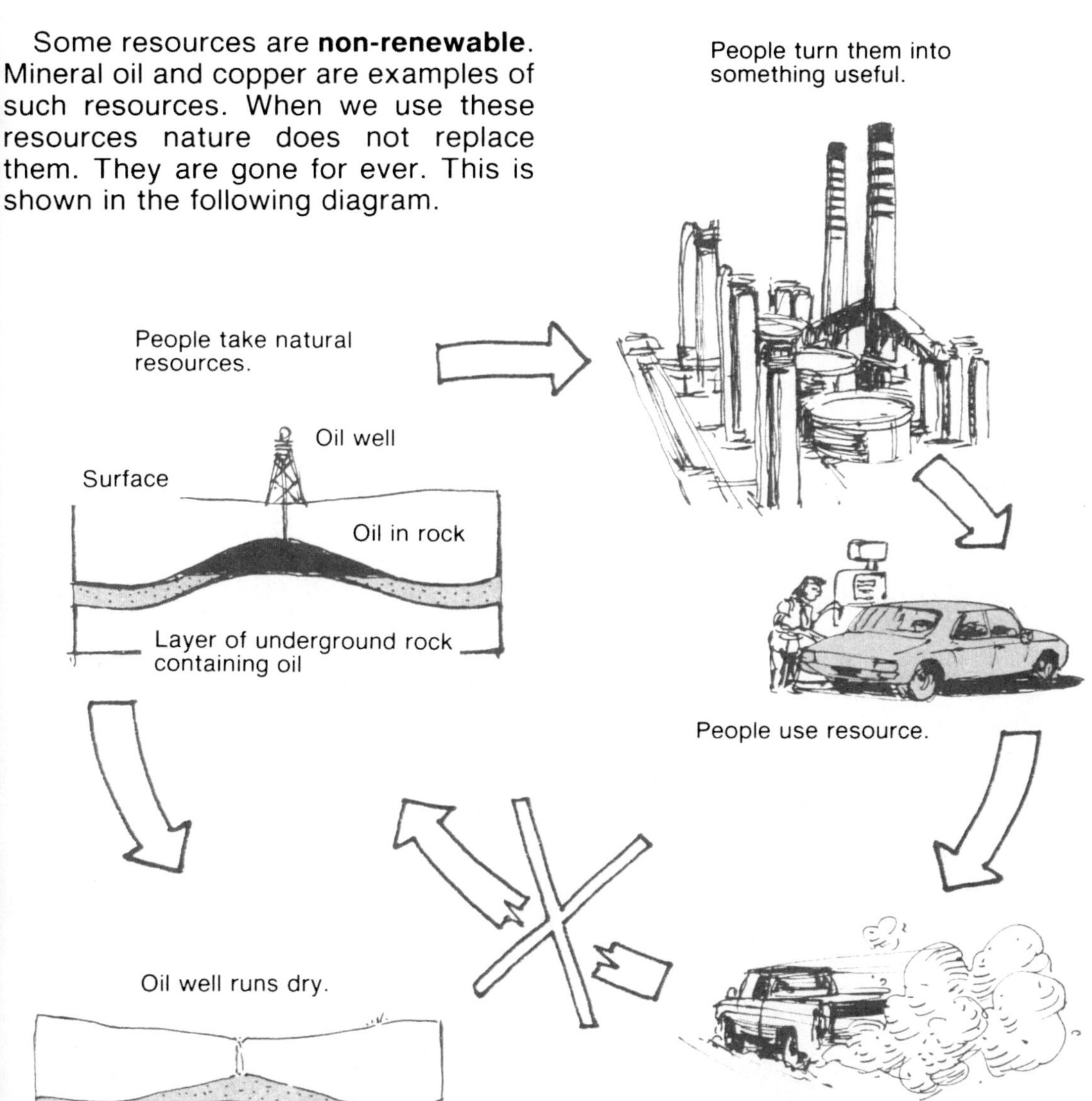

Petrol goes up in smoke.

The resource is used up.

One of the National Goals of Papua New Guinea's Constitution tells us to use and look after our resources carefully for the sake of our children, and our children's children. It states:

> We declare our fourth goal to be for Papua New Guinea's natural resources and environment to be conserved and used for the collective benefit of future generations.

This book is about the wise use of our resources.

Activities

Exercises

1. In your exercise books write down whether the following statements are TRUE (T) or FALSE (F):

   (a) Natural resources are useful to people.
   (b) Natural resources are made by people.
   (c) Renewable resources can be used only once.
   (d) There are no natural resources in the sea.
   (e) Minerals are a non-renewable resource.
   (f) Water is a renewable resource.
   (g) Trees should not be replanted after the forest is cut down.
   (h) Natural resources need to be carefully conserved and managed.
   (i) Only people who have been to school are useful human resources for society.
   (j) Human resources consist of all the people in a country.

2. Match the correct words with the descriptions:

manufacturing	resources found naturally in the environment
human resources	resources which can be used again
conservation	using our resources to make new things
renewable resources	resources made up of people's skills and knowledge.
natural resources	looking after the environment

3. Look around the classroom.
   (a) Make a list of things which have come from
   - renewable resources,
   - non-renewable resources.

   (b) Make a list of the things that the human resources in the school
   - could have manufactured themselves,
   - could not have manufactured themselves.

Using resources in the village.

4. Study the photograph on page 4.
   (a) What food resource is this boy looking for?
   (b) What things, shown on the photo, have the people who live here manufactured to make their life easier?
   (c) What natural resources did they use for this?

Things to discuss

1. Read again the extract from the Constitution.
   (a) What does "for the collective benefit of future generations" mean?
   (b) Why do you think the writers of the Constitution put in this goal?

Things to do

In small groups start a scrapbook on "Resources in Papua New Guinea". This project will take you the whole term. Collect pictures and newspaper clippings, or draw your own pictures and maps, and write your own articles. Divide your scrapbook into sections, and give each section a title. Some examples could be:

- Resources our grandparents used.
- Resources in the village.
- Resources of our province.
- Resources we send overseas.
- Resources we get from overseas.
- National parks.

At the end of term you will make displays in your classroom of the things you have done, so take care and do them well.

2. How People Use Their Resources

Using Resources

People can use resources without doing anything to them. An example of this is picking a coconut from its tree and eating it. However, coconuts are also used to make coconut oil. Coconuts in many areas of our country are grown to produce copra. This is the dried meat of the coconut. The copra is taken to factories here and overseas, where it is turned into coconut oil. Soap and margarine can be manufactured from coconut oil. Coconuts, therefore, can be used naturally or they can be processed to make things we need.

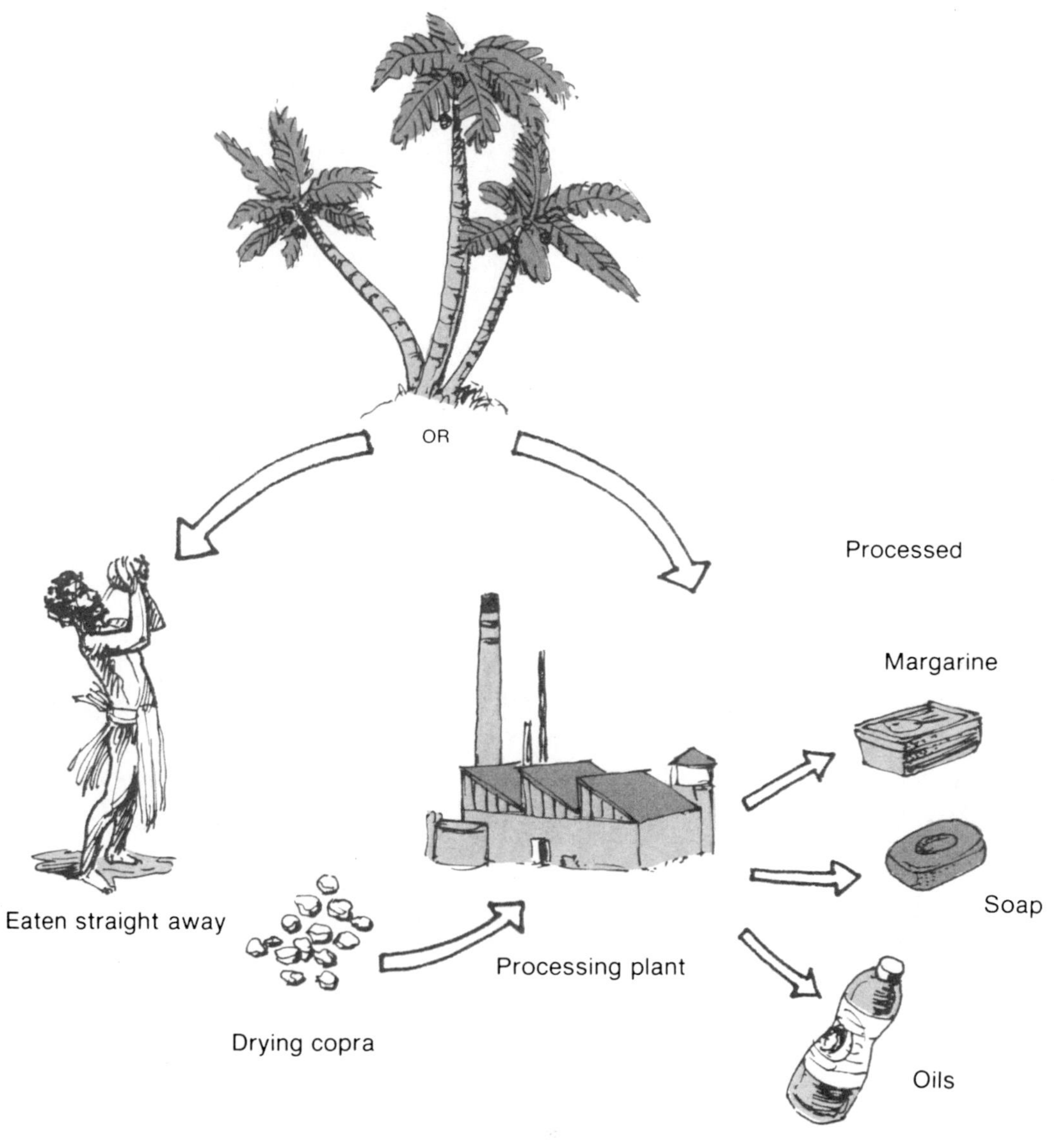

Study the diagram below:

Using what is around you.

A village on the Sepik River

The land near the village is used to grow bananas, kaukau and vegetables. After a few years, gardens are left fallow to rest the soil. Most of the crops that are grown are eaten by the people themselves. The waste is fed to pigs.

Strong branches from the forest are used for the frames of the huts and roof supports. Kunai grass is used to cover the roof. All of the materials used are found in the forest near the village. The people help each other to build new houses.

The forest also provides the people with some of their cultural needs. Bird of Paradise and hornbill feathers are used for bilas. Wood is used for carving masks. Mud from the river is used for colouring.

The river provides the people with water for drinking and washing. Fish, and sometimes crocodiles, are caught in the river. Both of these are an important food source. The river is also the main means of communication.

The forest also supplies the people with other sources of food. The men hunt wild pigs, bandicoots and birds in the forest. The women often collect wild breadfruit and pitpit.

The people in this community have the skills and knowledge to use their natural resources to support themselves. Older people pass these skills and knowledge on to the younger members of the community. Such a community is a truly **self-sufficient** one.

Trading Our Resources

Sometimes there are things that people want but cannot make themselves. For example, in the past, most communities needed stone tools to help them survive. Many did not have the resources or skills to make these tools. They had to trade their surplus resources with other communities for stone tools.

Today we need many things that we do not produce ourselves. Machinery, electrical goods, fuel and paper are examples. We buy these things from other countries. These things are called **imports**. The modern world needs many of the things we produce. Gold, copper, timber and coffee are some of the **exports** we send to other countries.

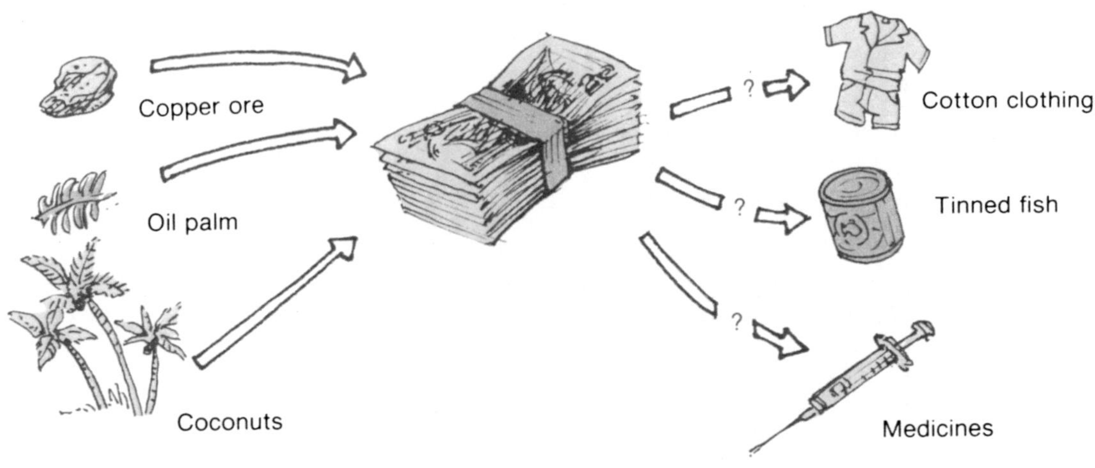

Resources sold for money to buy goods from other countries.

Papua New Guinea is a member of the world community. Different countries in the world **specialize** in producing different things. What they produce depends on their natural and human resources. They then trade for the things they need but do not produce themselves.

A good example of this is copper ore. Papua New Guinea has large reserves of copper ore, but we have no use for it. If we did not trade, then most of this copper ore would be of no value. However, West Germany uses a great deal of copper in its industries and has none of its own. It is to both Papua New Guinea's and West Germany's advantage that copper ore is mined here and sold to West Germany. The money from the sale of our copper ore helps to buy many of the things that we want.

Gold, copper, timber and coffee are some of the things that we export. Most of our exports are natural resources. Most of the things we import are manufactured goods which are produced using modern technology (see diagram above).

The map below shows some of our major trading relationships.

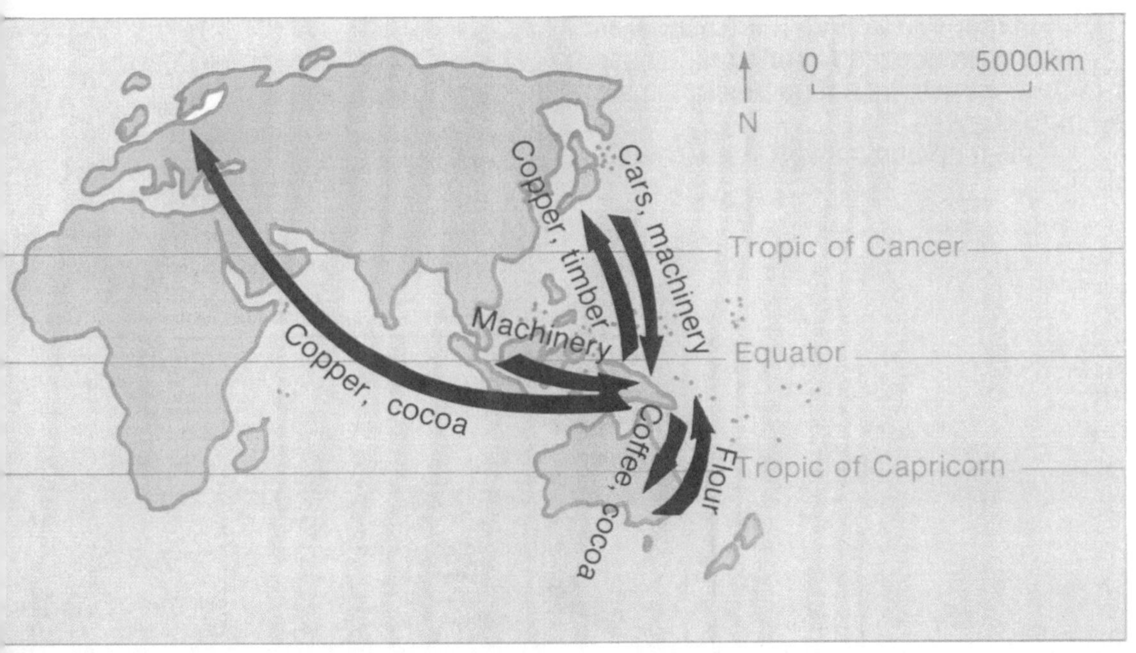

Map showing some of Papua New Guinea's main imports and exports.

Activities

Exercises

1. New skill

Most maps are divided into squares by thin lines called grid lines. These lines can help us to find places on the map quickly.

This map shows where Karo lives.

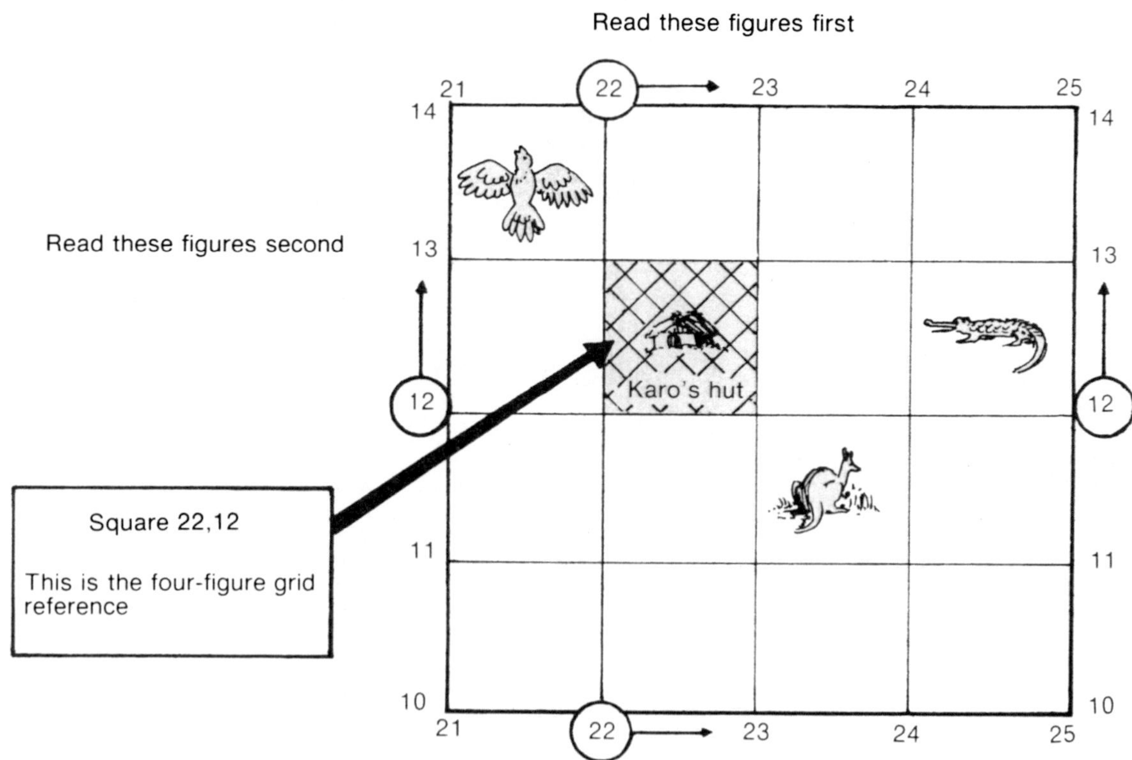

Karo lives in square 22.12. This is the square to the right of the vertical line labelled 22, and above the horizontal line labelled 12. This is a four-figure grid reference. This means that the bottom left corner of the square is where these two lines meet.

It is important always to read the vertical line first (the numbers at the top and bottom of the map), and the horizontal line second (the number at the right and left of the map.

Give the four-figure grid references where Karo could find

(a) the crocodile,
(b) the wallaby,
(c) the bird.

2. (a) Below is a map of the village which is described in the diagram on page 7. Study this map and the diagram, and then answer the following questions.

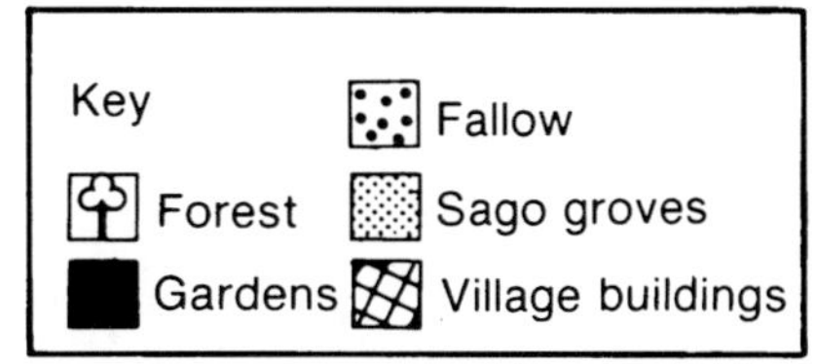

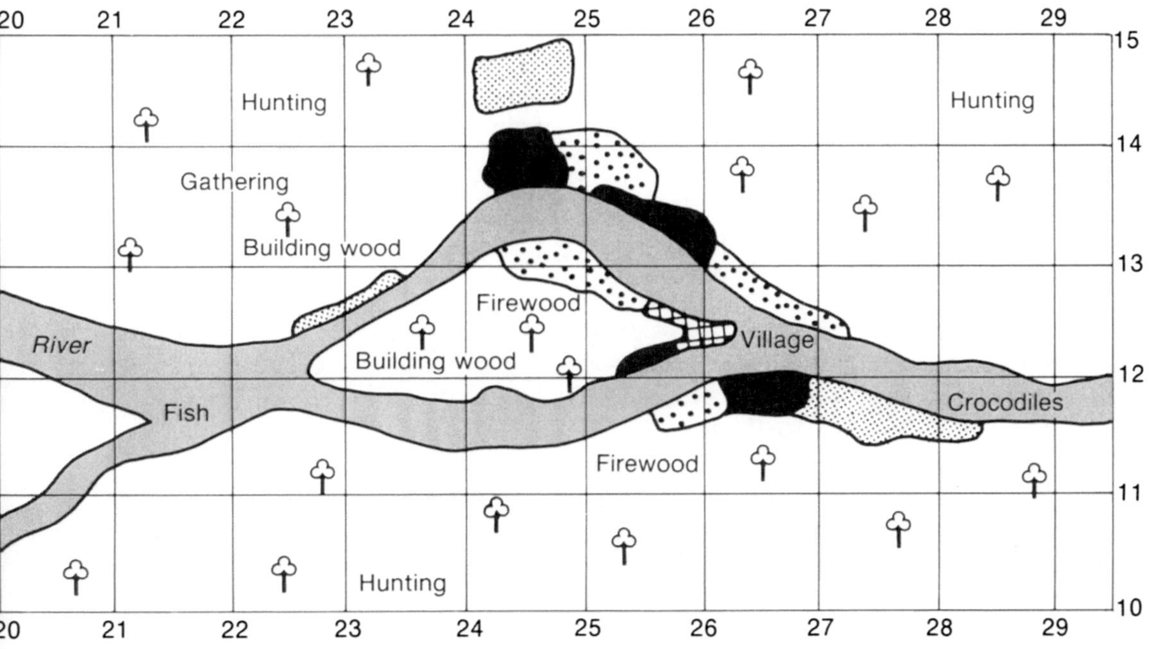

- What resources do the villagers get from the land?
- What resources do the villagers get from the river?
- Give the four-figure grid references for:
  - the two squares in which the village is found;
  - two squares where gardens are found;
  - the two squares in which most sago is found.
- What resources do you think the villagers produce to sell?
- How is the forest used? How does this use change the further you go from the village? Can you explain why this is?

(b) One boy, Seth, left the village to go to school, and is now studying at university. What skills will Seth
- gain by leaving the village and going to university?
- lose by leaving the village and going to university?

3. Study the map on page 26 of the *Papua New Guinea School Atlas* and answer these questions:

(a) What are the main resources of the Western Highlands?

(b) Name three provinces that produce rubber?

(c) In which two provinces is petroleum exploration taking place?

(d) How many tonnes of cocoa are being produced each year in the North Solomons?

(e) How many head of cattle are there in the whole of Papua New Guinea?

(f) Which are the three main timber-producing provinces?

4. Study the map on page 9 of this book and the one on page 48 of your atlas.

   (a) • To which two countries do most of our copper exports go?
   • Which country buys most of our coffee?
   • What kind of goods do we mostly import from Japan?
   • What country is the source of most of our imported foodstuffs?

   (b) Try to explain in your own words why trading with other countries is very important to Papua New Guinea.

Things to discuss

"Does the modern Papua New Guinean still need the traditional knowledge and skills of the village?"

Things to do

Draw a map of the area where you live, showing the resources you use and where you find them. Pupils in urban areas can do this too. Show the location of shops, markets, sports facilities, etc., that you use. You can add your own grid. Then test each other on finding places on each other's maps by using four-figure grid references.

3. Using the Land

Papua New Guineans think of the land as their most valuable resource. Unlike the majority of people in other countries of the world, most of our citizens have their own land. The land provides food, building materials, clothing, decorations, medicine, and tools. The land is a link with the past.

People have been living off this land for more than 50 000 years. Our people were skilled in agriculture at least 10 000 years ago. The remains of drainage ditches discovered at the tea plantations at Kuk in the Waghi Valley prove this. Some scientists believe that Papua New Guinea may be the birthplace of agriculture.

The Soil

Much of the land in the world is covered by a thin layer of soil. Soil is a mixture of broken-down rock and the remains of dead plants and animals. This mixture provides the food needed for plants to grow.

A soil which is good for growing plants is called a fertile soil. Not all soils in Papua New Guinea are fertile. The most fertile soils are found in the valleys of the Central Highlands, and around volcanoes in the coastal areas. Volcanic ash makes very fertile soil because it adds many useful minerals to the soil.

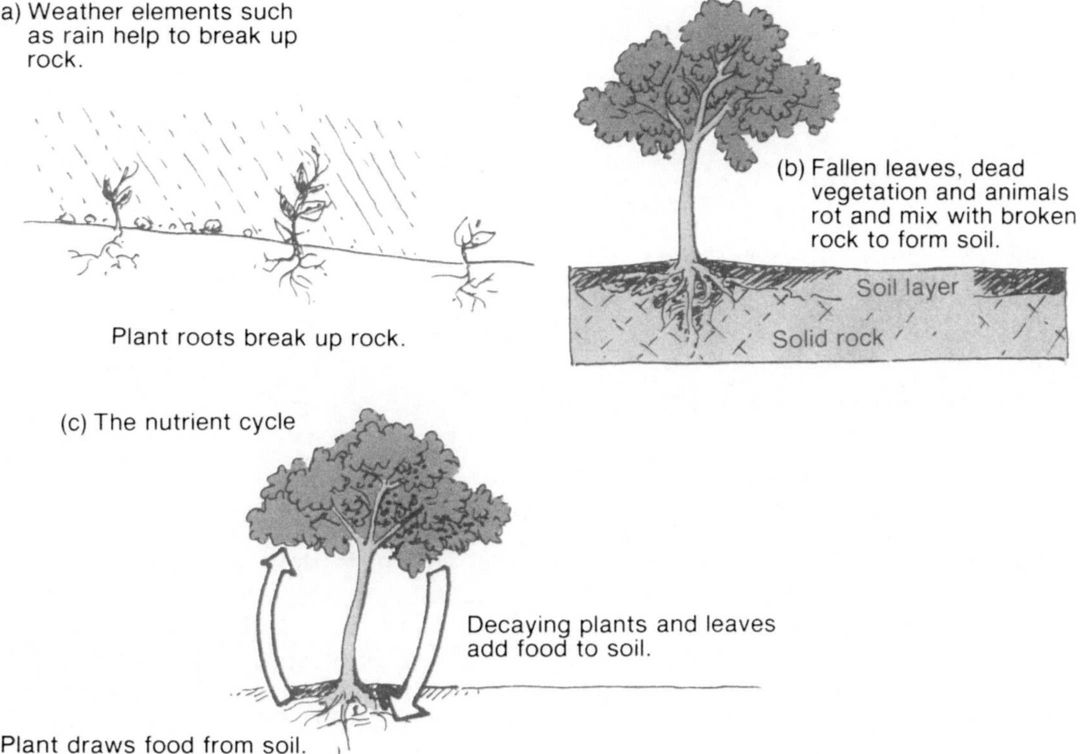

Soil formation and use.

Growing Food

The map below shows the main food crops in different areas of Papua New Guinea.

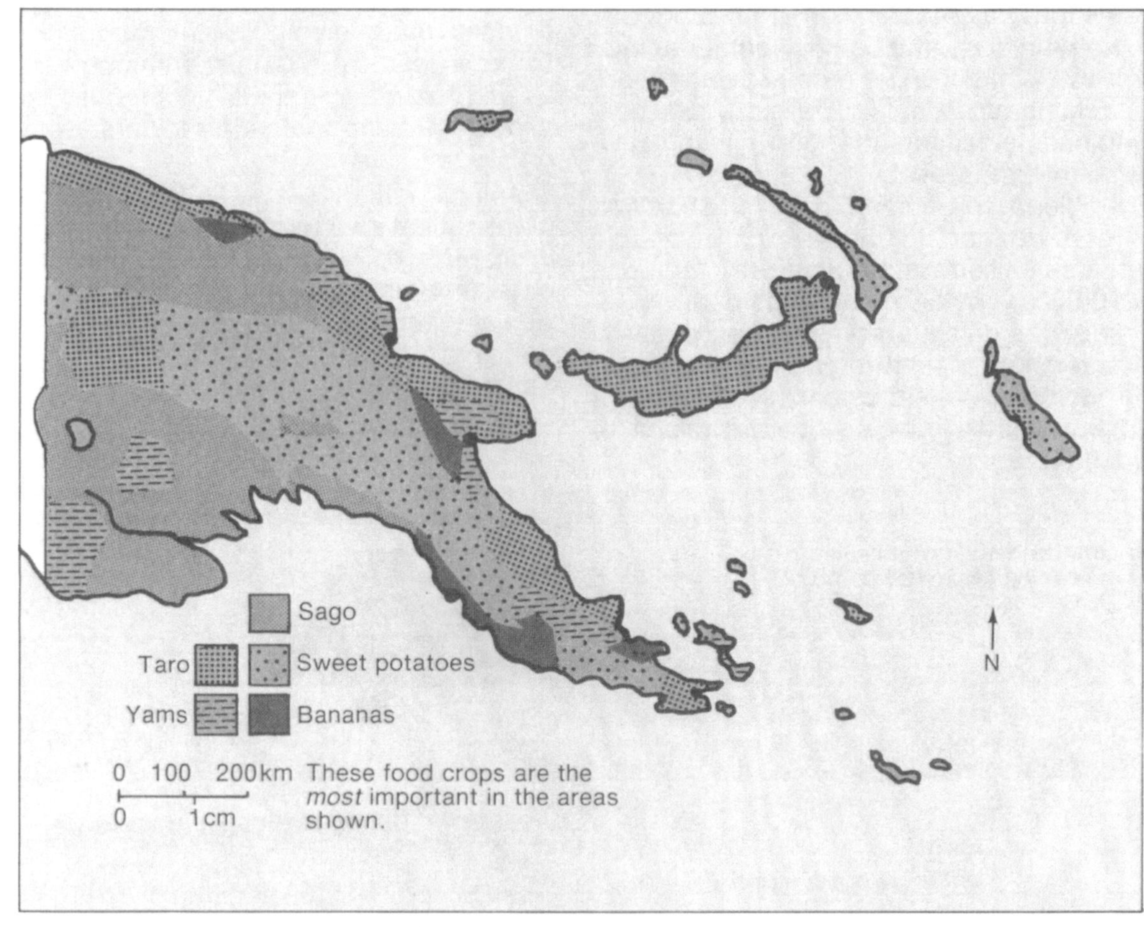

Main food crops of Papua New Guinea.

We must look after the soil so that we can have successful agriculture. More than 80 per cent of Papua New Guineans are subsistence farmers. The system used by these farmers depends on the kind of soil, the slope of the land and the climate. In every part of the world, successfully growing food crops depends on the suitability of the land and the climate. The next map shows the main agricultural areas of the world. It also shows the main types of foods produced.

People in Papua New Guinea recognize the value of soil, and have developed methods to protect and keep it healthy. They have found ways of making sure that the soil is not washed away, and that the **nutrients** used up by plants are put back into the soil.

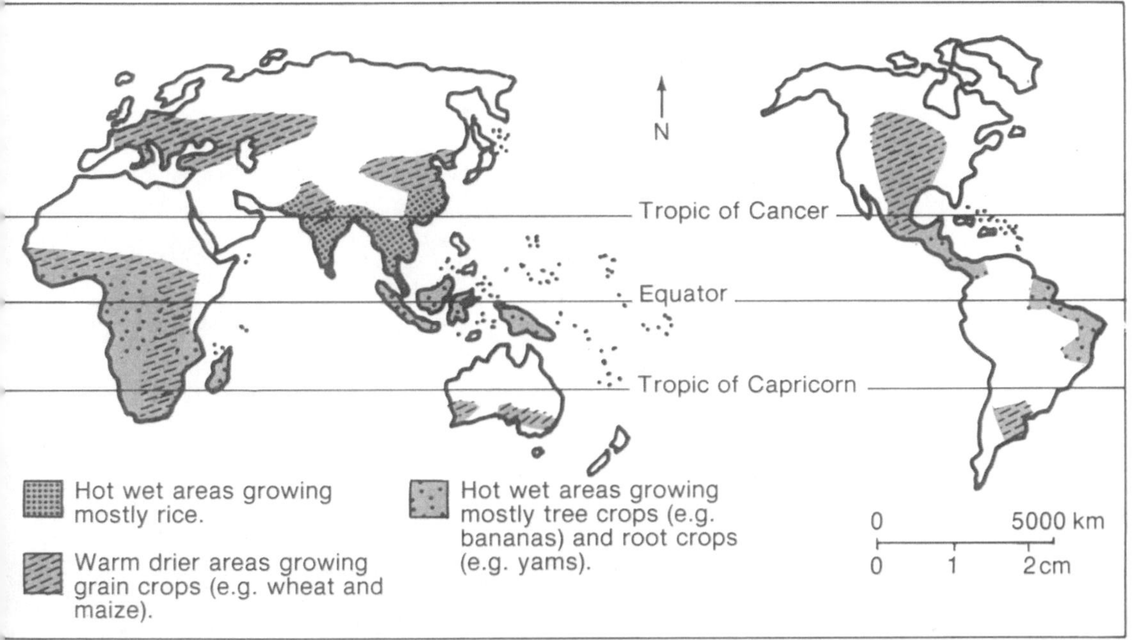

Some of the major food crop areas in the world.

Lowland Gardening and Shifting Agriculture

In the lowland swamps the people gather sago and other food plants from the bush. There are usually only a few gardens. In some swamp areas farmers have developed systems of drainage to enable them to grow more food. Taro is a suitable crop for swampy areas.

Swamp drainage and taro gardens near Tari, Southern Highlands Province.

Extracting sago from the palm.

In the lowland forest areas the people use a system of shifting cultivation. They make gardens by clearing the forest. Then they dry and burn the plants they have cut down and spread the ash on the land they have cleared. This helps to make the soil more **fertile**.

Stopping soil erosion by using tree trunks, Goodenough Island, Milne Bay Province.

These gardeners grow crops on an area of land for one or two years. Then they move to a new area and clear more forest. When land is cultivated, the plants remove **nutrients** from the soil, and it becomes less fertile. By moving to new gardens, the people make sure that the soil is left unused or fallow. If the fallow time is long enough the nutrients will be replaced. The land may then be used again. As the number of people in an area increases, the fallow time often gets shorter. If the fallow time is not long enough then the soil will not recover and the gardener will find that his next crop will not grow properly. Shifting cultivation can continue if there is plenty of land and not too many gardeners.

Highlands Gardening

The forests in the valleys of the Highlands have long since disappeared because of man's farming activities. Sweet potato is now the most important crop here. **Erosion** is always a problem in these steep gardens. This is because the soil is washed away down the slopes during periods of heavy rain. The gardeners here use logs, fences and deep ditches to protect the soil from this erosion. Trees such as the casuarina, whose roots add nutrients to the soil, are often planted around gardens.

Wooden fences used to stop soil erosion in Chimbu Province.

Commercial Farming

Cash crops

People have always traded their extra food crops for things they did not have. Goods (such as steel tools, cloth and imported food), and services (such as education and transport) are all part of life today.

To get the money to buy these things, many people grow crops to sell, as well as for their own food. Almost 90 per cent of village people grow some crops for sale.

The subsistence gardeners who live in the villages around Port Moresby now grow many crops to sell in the city markets. Coconuts, bananas, green leaves, sweet potatoes, paw-paws, pineapples, mangoes, and spring onions, are examples of food crops grown for sale. These gardeners provide a very useful service to the town people who do not have the land to grow their own food.

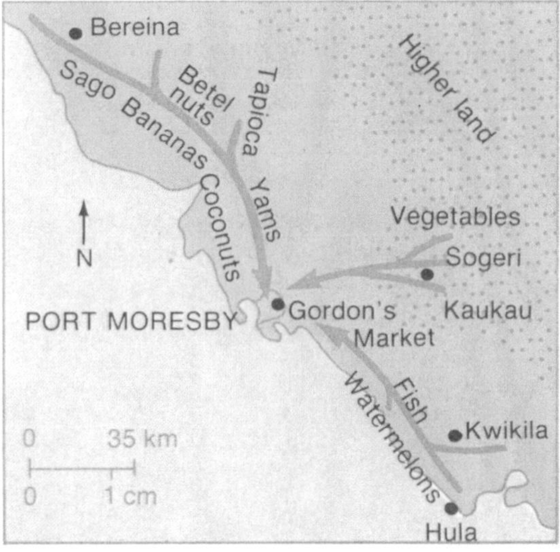

Some of the crops sold in Gordon's Market, Port Moresby, come from these areas.

Gordon's Market, Port Moresby.

Plantations

Plantations were set up in most of the tropical areas the Europeans **colonized**. They were established to grow crops which could not be grown in the colder climate of Europe. The produce from these plantations fetched high prices. They were owned and run by European companies. Plantations usually concentrated on only one crop, all of which was exported.

Some of the first European settlers in Papua New Guinea came to take advantage of our rich soils and to grow such crops. The German government in New Guinea encouraged the establishment of large plantations, especially in East New Britain, New Ireland, North Solomons, Manus and Madang. Some Australian plantations were also set up in Papua.

Coconuts, cocoa and rubber were the most successful plantation crops grown in coastal areas. Later coffee became important in the Highlands region. Plantations, like the one shown below, were, and still are, important employers of our people.

A coconut plantation in East New Britain Province.

Splitting coconuts to obtain the meat for copra.

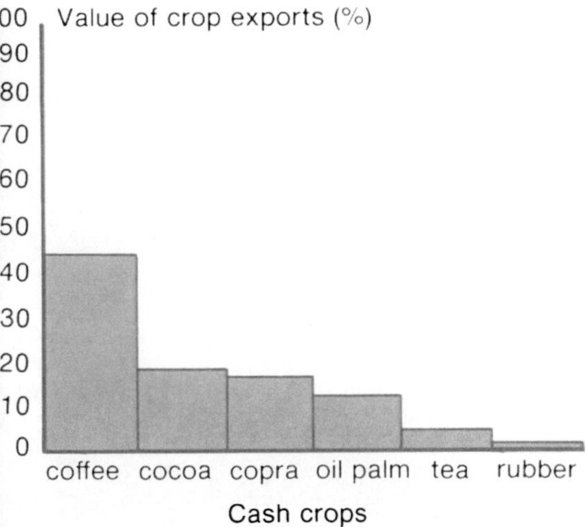

Cash crop exports.

Since Independence in 1975 the government has assisted village people to buy plantations owned by foreigners. The government also helps the new owners to run their plantations. However, some plantations are still owned by foreign companies. The export of cash crops is a very important part of our economy. The column graph above shows the value of cash crop exports.

Small-holder agriculture

Our people saw the importance of the new crops and began to grow them on their own land. As early as 1910, the majority of copra exported from Papua New Guinea came from villages. Today small-scale village growers produce a major part of all our important cash crops. Village growers produce more than twice as much coffee and cocoa as they grow in big plantations. The graph below shows the 1983 production for the main cash crops in both small-holder blocks and big plantations.

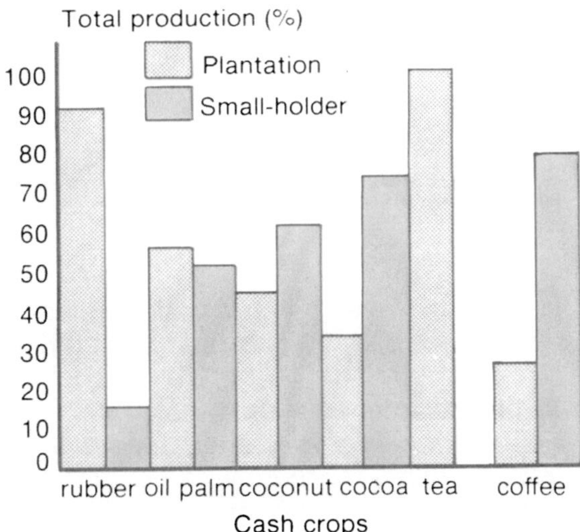

Nucleus estates

In recent years the plantation and the small-holder systems of agriculture have been combined. In this system, a central plantation called a **nucleus estate** is surrounded by many small-holder blocks.

An example is the first oil palm plantation established in 1967 at Hoskins in West New Britain. There, the nucleus estate is a large foreign-owned plantation. This plantation also has a mill to process the fruits of the oil palm trees and produce high quality oil for export. Many small-holders own blocks of oil palms on land around the main plantation. These small-holders are called **outgrowers**.

This diagram shows the main idea of the nucleus estate scheme.

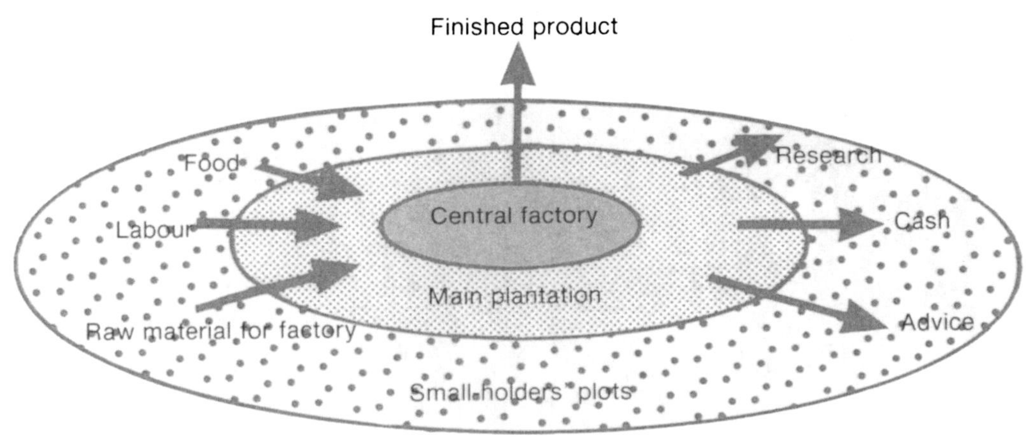

A nucleus estate system.

The small-holders work their blocks with the help of the skilled staff from the nucleus estate. They sell their produce to the nucleus estate.

The scheme is a way of getting cash crops grown and processed at low cost by village people, using modern agricultural methods.

As well as the Hoskins estate, there are oil palm nucleus estates at Bialla (also in West New Britain), Popondetta in Oro Province, and Alotau in the Milne Bay Province. The sugar plantations at Ramu in Madang Province, and the rubber plantations at Cape Rodney in Central Province and at Gavien in East Sepik Province, also use the nucleus estate system.

Because the land is being used to grow one crop year after year, cash crop farming is very different from subsistence agriculture. For the best results, chemicals, such as fertilizers and insecticides, are needed. Fertilizers provide plant foods while insecticides help to kill pests that cause plant diseases.

These chemicals are expensive, and small-holders sometimes cannot afford to use them.

Small-holder getting his crop ready for collection by the trucks from the oil palm mill, Hoskins, West New Britain Province.

Sterilizing the oil palm nuts before crushing at the Mosa oil palm mill, Kimbe, West New Britain Province.

The Future

The land and its soil are probably our most valuable natural resources. The land has supported us and our ancestors for many thousands of years. Both are now in danger and will continue to support us only if we use them wisely.

The resources available for hunting, fishing and gathering are decreasing. As our population increases, more land is required to grow food. Small-holders are now producing more and more of our cash crops. Food crops and cash crops are competing for the best land. Already, in some parts of the country, the best land is being used for growing cash crops. Food production is being pushed to the less fertile land.

Many people now have money to buy food. The replacement foods we buy, such as rice and tinned fish, sometimes do not give us a balanced and healthy diet.

There are many arguments about the way our agricultural land should be used. Some people believe that commercial farming and cash crops should be developed. Other people believe that Papua New Guinea should concentrate on subsistence farming. We need to understand both these arguments.

Activities

Exercises

1. Write sentences to answer the following questions:
   (a) What is soil?
   (b) How is soil formed?
   (c) Where are the best soils found in Papua New Guinea?
2. Using the maps of food crops in both Papua New Guinea and the world on pages 14 and 15 and the *Papua New Guinea School Atlas* to help you, complete the two tables opposite.
   (a) What is the major food crop you would expect to see growing in the countryside around the following towns and cities?

Papua New Guinea	Other countries of the world
Daru	Chicago (USA)
Goroka	Beijing (China)
Rabaul	Guangchou (China)
Lae	Moscow (USSR)
Wewak	Calcutta (India)
Alotau	Kinshasa (Zaire)
Arawa	Nairobi (Kenya)

   (b) From what you have read so far, complete the table below and copy it into your exercise book.

Environment	Food crop you would grow	Ways to manage the soil
Lowland swamp		
Highland slopes		

3. In small groups, carefully study the map below.

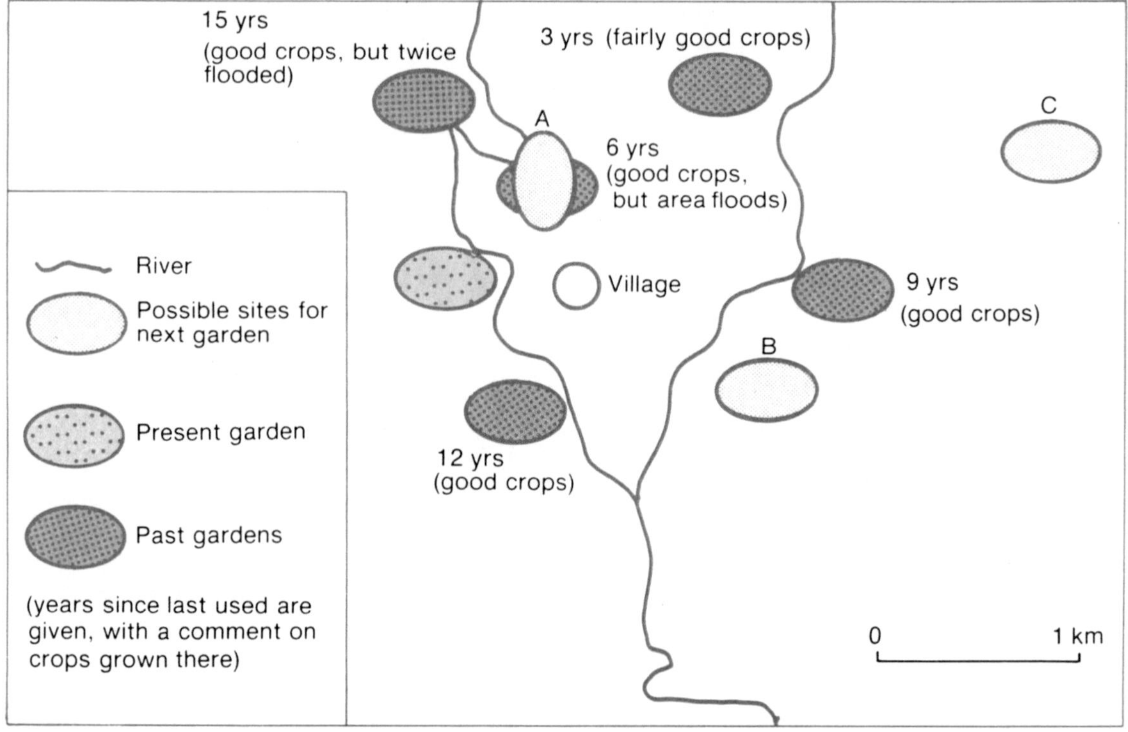

Shifting cultivation.

Which land to use next?

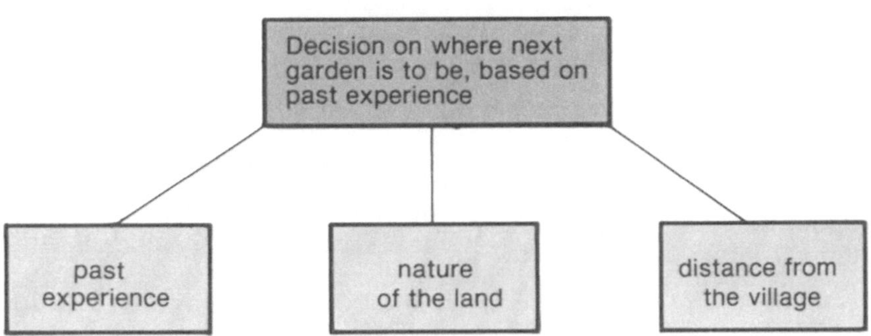

(a) Imagine you are villagers here. You have to decide where your next year's garden is to be. You have three choices: sites A, B and C. Using the information on the map and the text:
- discuss and then write down the advantages and disadvantages of each site.
- state which one you would choose.

(b) From the words in the list below, fill in the blanks:

two, regains, traditional, forest, again, fertility, new, fallow, subsistence.

Shifting cultivation is the ____________ method of protecting soil ____________. It is used by ____________ gardeners. In this method the gardener grows crops on a piece of land for about ____________ years, and then the garden is moved to a ____________ area, where the ____________ is cleared and new crops are planted. By moving the garden around the people make sure that the soil ____________ its fertility, and it may be used ____________ after some years. When land is left like this, it is called ____________ land.

4. (a) Explain what is meant by the following:
- fertile soil
- erosion
- nutrients
- subsistence farming
- commercial farming.

(b)
- Explain the difference between plantations, small-holdings and nucleus estates.
- What are the advantages of the nucleus estate system?

5. Study the bar graphs on page 19. Answer the following questions:

(a) Which is the least important cash crop?

(b) Which is the most important?

(c) What share of total crop exports has the most important cash crop?

(d) Which cash crop is grown totally on plantations?

(e) Which cash crop is mostly grown by small-holders?

Things to do

Collect more pictures and articles for your scrapbook. Look in the newspapers for articles on agriculture and cash crops in Papua New Guinea. If you belong to a farming community, make a section in your scrapbook on farming decisions in your village, and how they were made.

4. Water as a Resource

Our planet Earth is a watery world. If you look at a photograph of the Earth taken from a spaceship or a satellite, you will see that it is mainly blue. In fact, two-thirds of the Earth's surface is covered by water.

Water is essential for life. If there was no more rain, the ground would dry out. Plants would die, and our valuable soil would be blown away in great dust storms. Soon all animals, including people, would also die. An earth without water would be a very different planet.

The Water Cycle

Water is everywhere around us. There is water in the seas, on the land and in the air.

The oceans lose water through evaporation. They also gain water which flows back into them in rivers or through spaces in the rocks or through the soil. The movement of water from the sea to the atmosphere, then falling as rain, and flowing back to the sea again, is known as the water cycle. Water is a renewable resource.

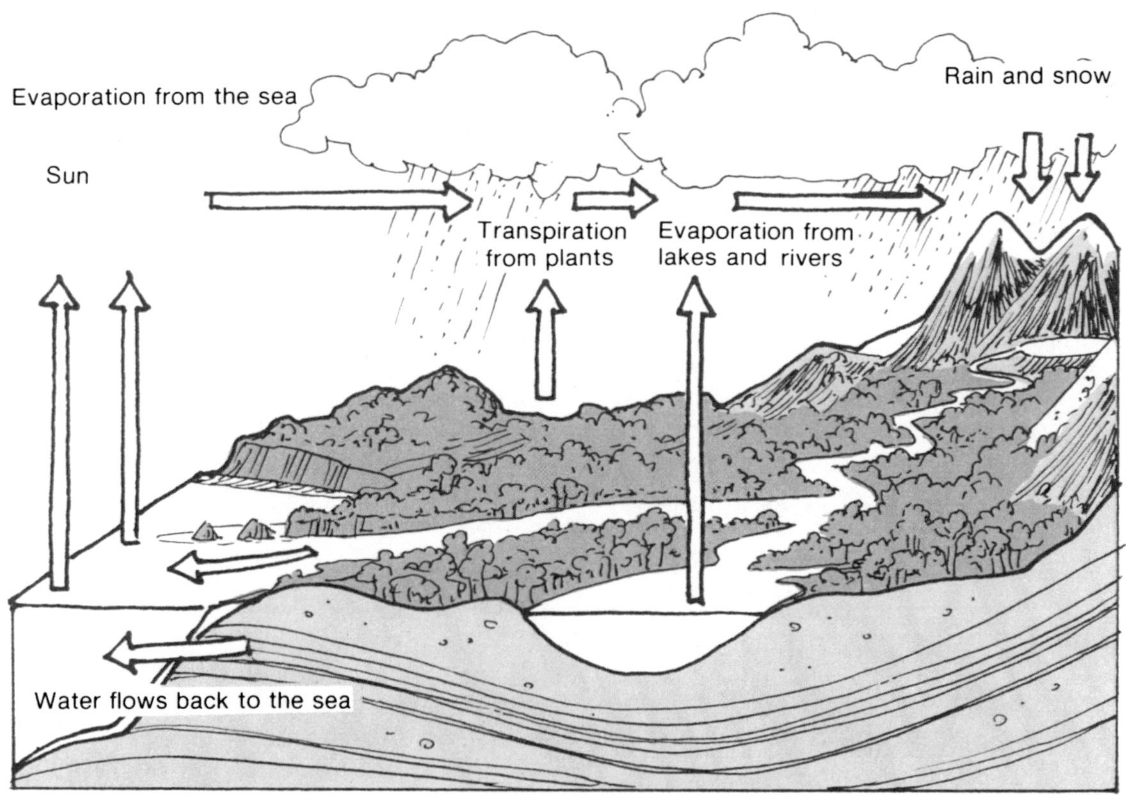

The water cycle.

Fresh Water

In Papua New Guinea there often seems to be plenty of water, both as rainfall and in the rivers. However, some areas have a heavier rainfall than others. Look at the two graphs below.

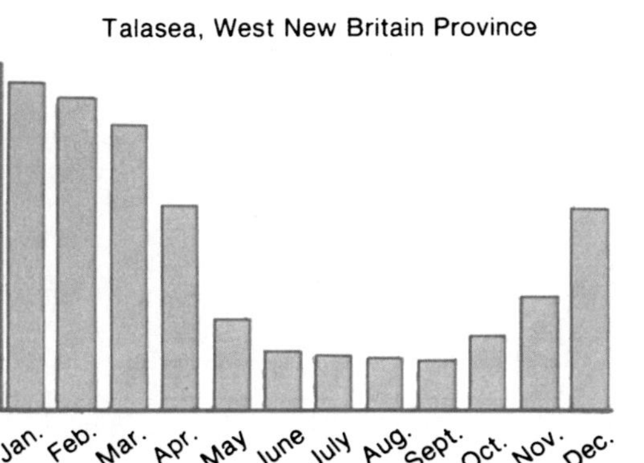

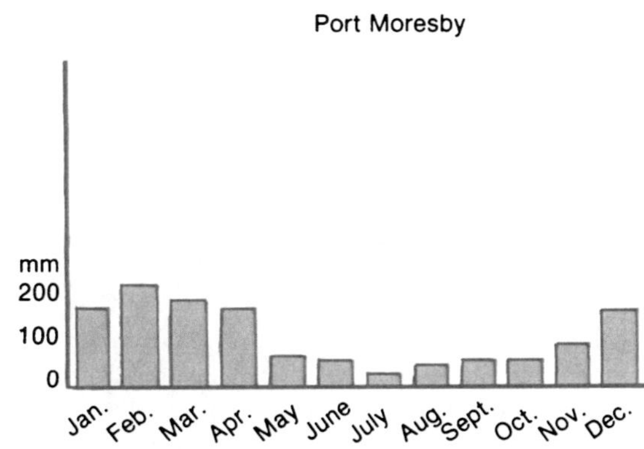

Average rainfall figures.

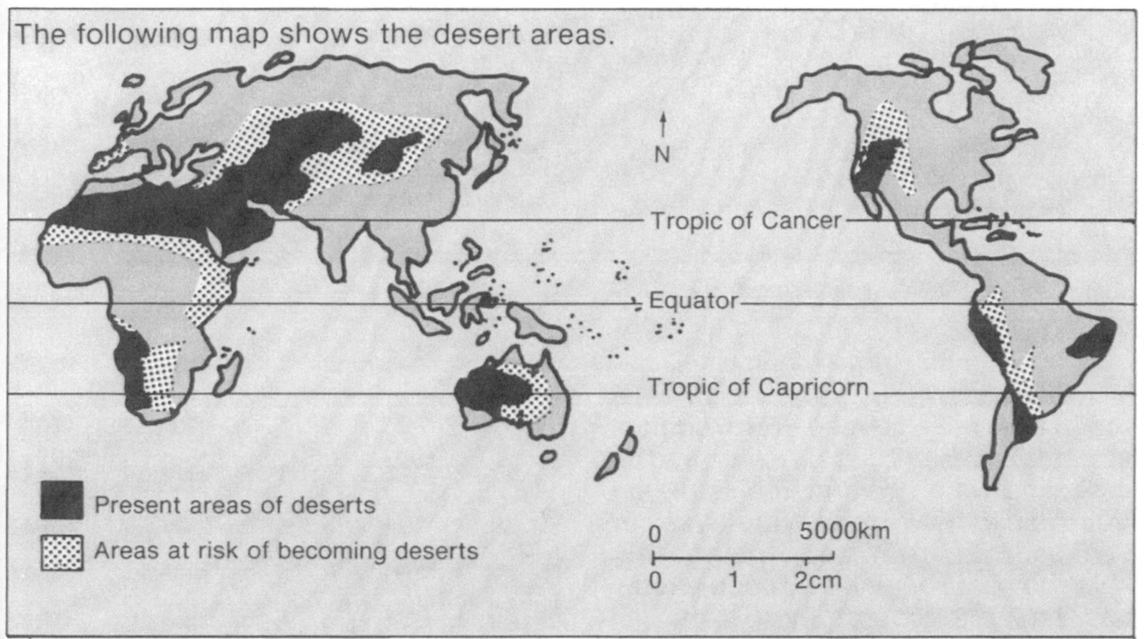

Land at risk of becoming deserts.

Some places in the world have very little rain. Large parts of Central Australia, North Africa, and other regions of the Earth's surface, are deserts. These are very dry areas where few plants grow. Many other areas suffer from long periods without rain (called droughts).

Ethiopians drive their herd along a dried-up river bed at Degabur in Ethiopia's Ogaden Desert. ▷

Because of the high central mountains and heavy rainfall in Papua New Guinea there are many rivers. The map below shows the main rivers.

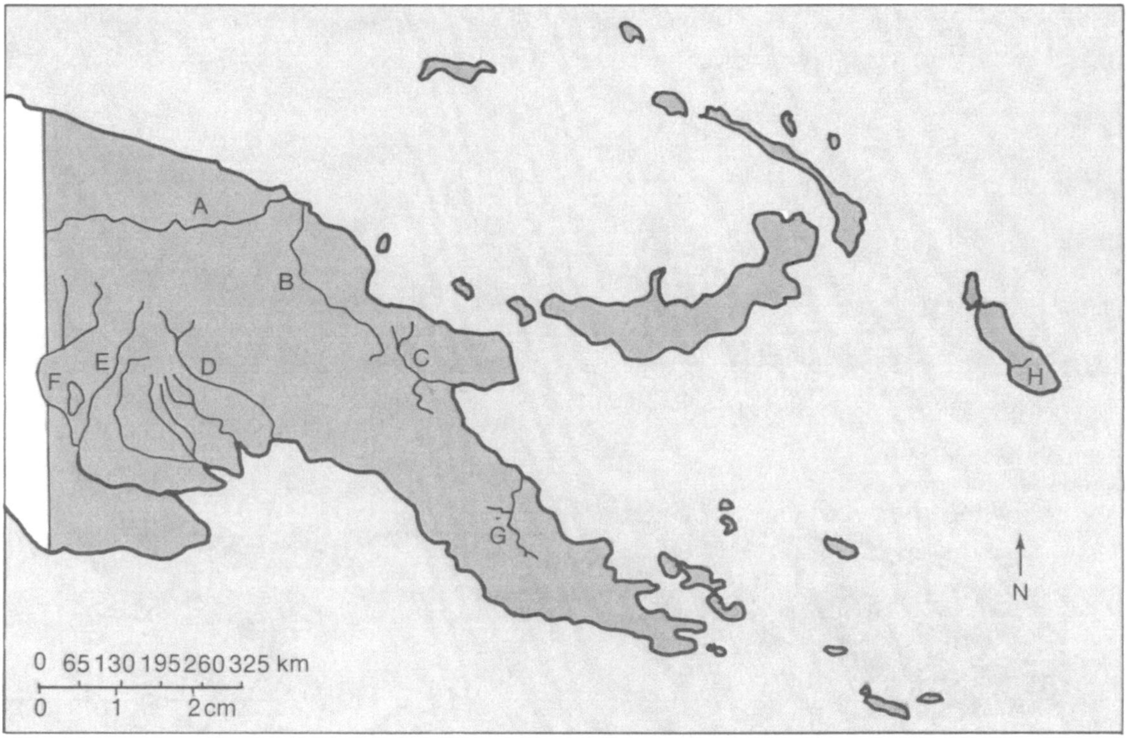

Some of Papua New Guinea's major rivers.

Traditionally, our people obtained the water they needed from springs, streams, rivers, ponds, wells, and by collecting water from house roofs and trees during heavy rain. Water was carried and stored in pots, gourds and bamboo containers. Many people today use tanks to collect and store rain water. Man-made lakes, called **reservoirs**, are used to collect and store water for Port Moresby and other large towns.

Over 80 per cent of deaths from disease are caused by germs in water. There are strong traditional taboos against the **pollution** of drinking water.

Sirinumu Dam, Central Province.

Town water supplies today are filtered and treated with special chemicals to make them safe to drink.

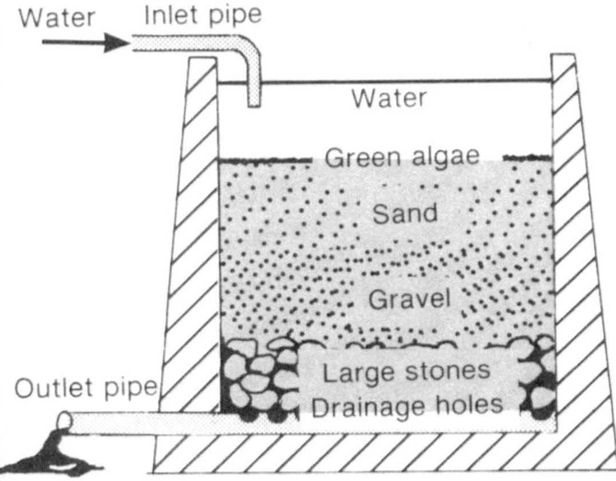

A simple water filtration plant.

Plants need water to grow. The most common source of water for plants is from rainfall. Rain, however, does not always fall when the farmer needs it. Many farmers in the world bring water from rivers and lakes to their gardens to make sure the plants get the water they need. Using water, other than rainfall, to help crops to grow is called **irrigation**. Many of our people in the past have used irrigation to water their crops during the dry season. Some use bamboo pipelines and drains to carry water to their gardens. Today many farmers use electric pumps to do this.

Resources from Water

Many of our people live near rivers, lakes or the sea. Their ways of life are closely linked to water. Fish, turtles, crabs and many different kinds of shellfish are a good source of food. There are many different traditional ways of catching fish. Some people use nets, some hooks and lines, others bows and arrows. In some areas derris root is used as a poison to stun the fish and bring them to the surface of the water. Many fishermen today use modern steel hooks and nylon nets, and fish from boats with outboard motors.

River-fishing using a net, Western Province.

Japanese tuna fishermen, New Ireland Province.

Commercial Fishing

Today fishing is a very important commercial industry. Large quantities of barramundi, mud crabs, crayfish and prawns are caught by village fishermen for sale here and overseas.

Shells are also important and are used for decoration and as traditional money. Crocodiles are now bred in farms in many parts of the country. They are an important source of money for many village people because their skins sell for high prices overseas.

Special ships with large freezers come to fish in the seas around Papua New Guinea. These ships come mainly from Japan, the United States of America and Taiwan. They catch mainly tuna, crayfish and prawns. The fishermen freeze their catch on board the ship and take it back to their own country for sale. Many thousands of tonnes are caught each year.

There is some danger that the numbers of fish in the waters around Papua New Guinea will become much smaller in the near future. As a result of this, in 1979 our government claimed the fishing rights to the area of sea up to 325 kilometres from the coastline. Other countries who want to fish in these waters now have to pay our government. The patrol boats of the Defence Force guard our waters and arrest any ships which fish there without permission.

We export fresh fish. We also import large amounts of tinned mackerel. Tinned fish have become an important part of the diet of many people, especially those in towns and government institutions such as schools.

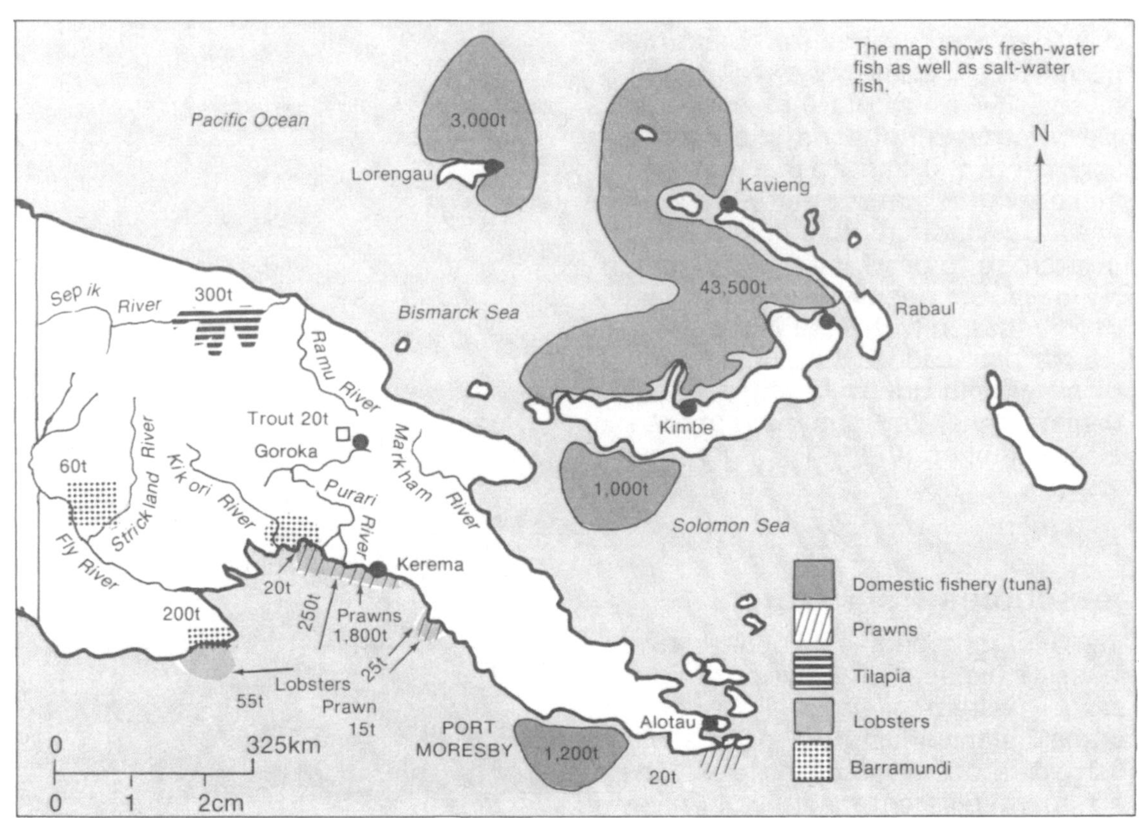

A map showing the yearly commercial fish catch.

Hydro-electricty

The energy of our fast-flowing rivers can be changed into useful electricity by hydro-electric power generators. Most of Port Moresby's electricity comes from hydro-electric power stations along the Laloki River. Other hydro-electric power stations in the Eastern Highlands and East New Britain Provinces provide electric power to the Highlands, Madang and Rabaul. Some plantations, mission settlements, and even villages, use small hydro-electric generators to make electric power.

So the water used is a renewable resource. We also save money because we do not have to burn expensive fuels like oil and gas.

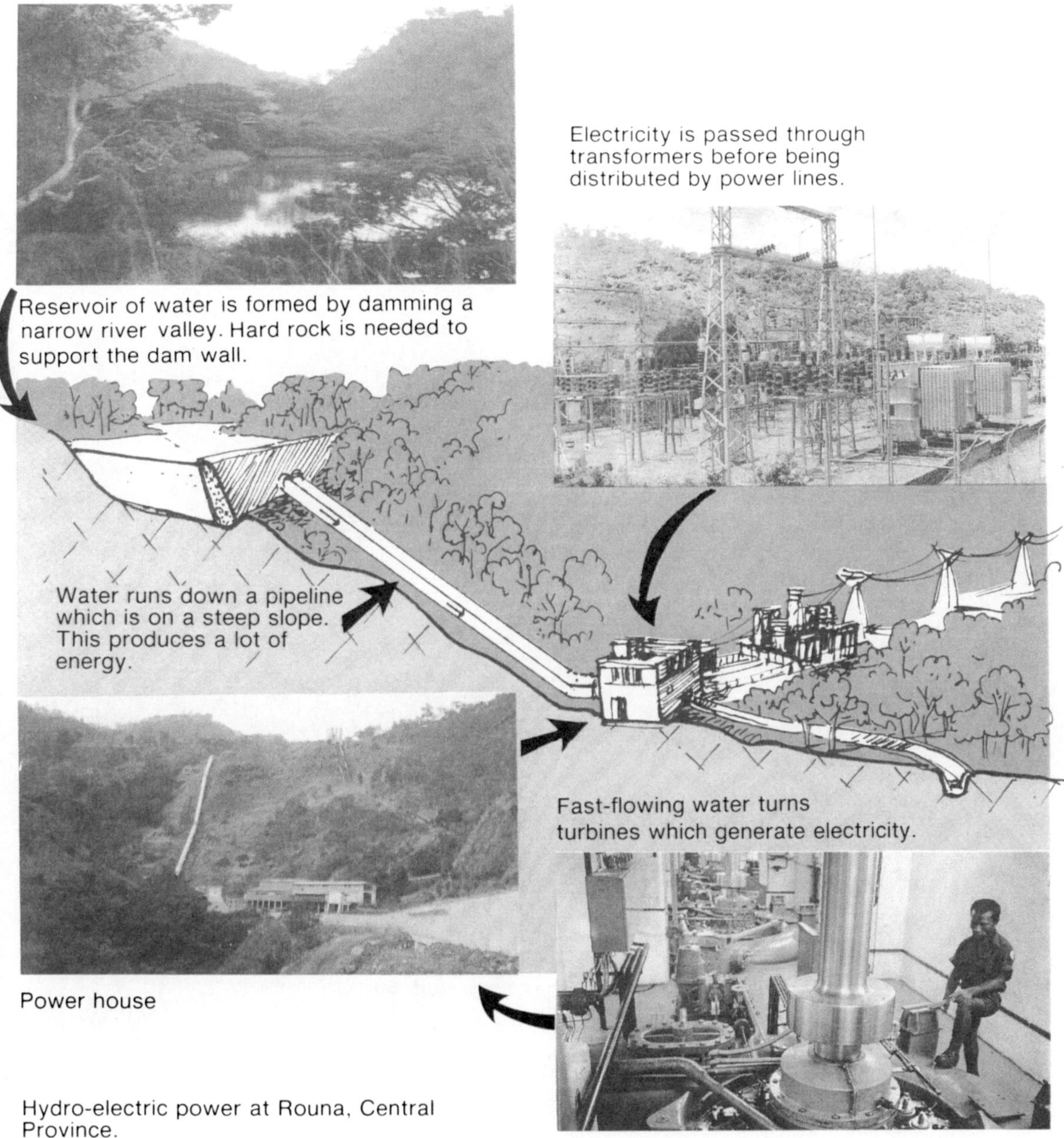

Hydro-electric power at Rouna, Central Province.

There are many other ways in which water is now used as a resource in Papua New Guinea. Transport and tourism are two of these.

Transport

The rivers and seas of Papua New Guinea are important for travel. Many of our early ancestors came to this region in sailing boats. Canoe-building and sailing are traditional skills. Coastal and river children use canoes from a very early age. Canoes are still very important for fishing and transport.

Today ships and barges serve all major coastal and river centres. Ocean-going ships transport most of our imports and exports.

Tourism

Tourists from many parts of the world visit Papua New Guinea. Some come to our warm climate to relax and enjoy the natural beauty of our beaches, clean blue seas, and coral reefs. Others come to enjoy the excitement of canoeing on our fast-flowing rivers. Tourism could become a major industry in the future, as it has in many parts of the Pacific area. This will happen only if foreigners feel that they can travel safely through our country.

White-water rafting in Papua New Guinea.

Activities

Exercises

The water cycle.

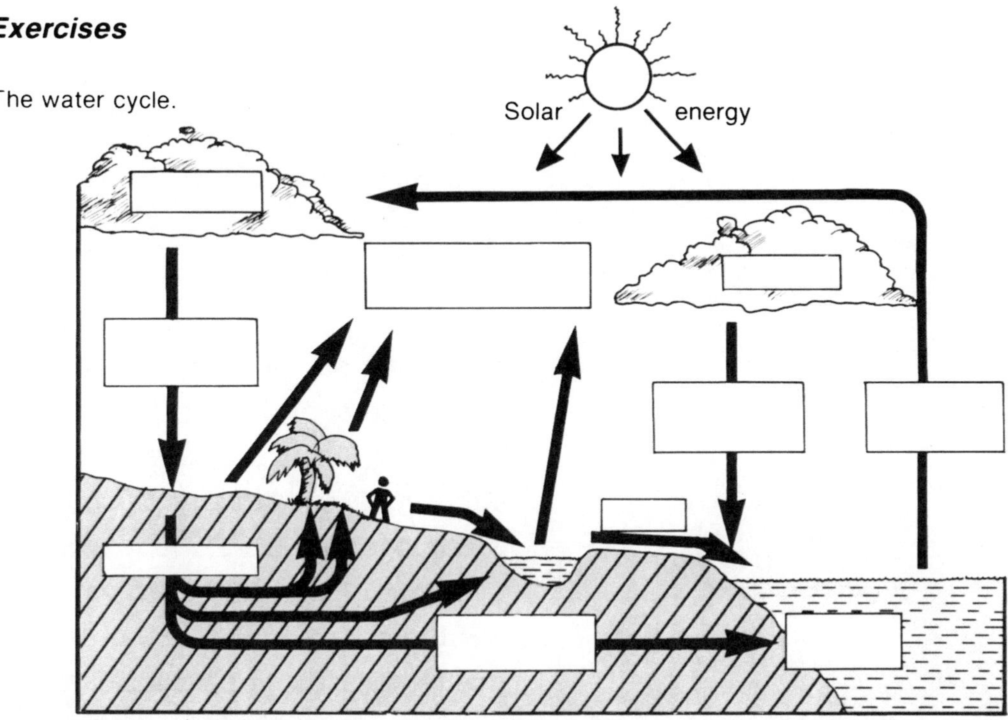

Key Which box has which letter? Some are used more than once.

A Evaporation

B Condensation

C Rainfall

D Some water runs on the surface

E Some water sinks into the ground

F Some groundwater flows back to the sea

G The sea

1. **(a)** Copy the diagram of the water cycle and of the key. Put the correct letters from the key in the appropriate boxes on the diagram.
   (b) Explain why it is called a "cycle".
2. Study the rainfall graphs for Port Moresby and Talasea.
   (a) For each place state
   - the total rainfall;
   - the wettest month;
   - the driest month.

   (b) What problem associated with rainfall might occur
   - in Port Moresby?
   - in Talasea?
3. Study the world map on page 25.
   (a) Using the *Papua New Guinea School Atlas*, name one country in each continent which has a large area of desert.
   (b) What does the map on page 25 of this book tell us about the world's deserts? Can you suggest a reason why this is happening?
4. Using your atlas, name the rivers that are shown by letters on the map on page 26 of this book (you will need to use the regional maps of Papua New Guinea to do this).

5. Draw a diagram like the one below to show the different ways in which we use water and the resources we get from it. (You could do this on a large piece of paper and display it on the wall. It could be illustrated with examples from your area.)

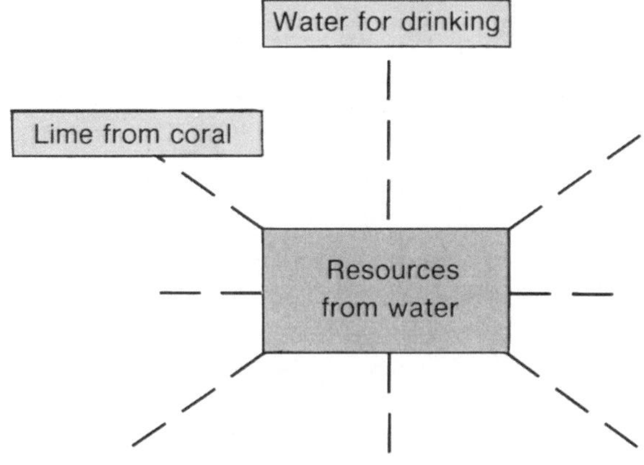

6. Study the map of fishing areas on page 28. Answer the following:
   (a) • Where is the largest area of commercial fishing in Papua New Guinea? How many tonnes of fish are caught there each year?
   • In which Province are most barramundi fish caught?
   • What is the main fish caught in the Sepik River?
   • Where are most of the shellfish (lobsters and prawns) caught?
   (b) • What is the main advantage of allowing ships from other countries to fish in our waters?
   • Why does the government have to be careful, when allowing this to take place? (The photographs on page 27 might help you to answer this question.)

7. From the words in the list below fill in the blanks:

   coal, powerlines, rainfall, pipeline, transformers, strong, steep, clean, energy, reservoirs, fast, turbine, renewable, power house, electricity.

   Hydro-electric power is very important in Papua New Guinea. The high ____________, and ____________ mountain slopes in much of the country, create a lot of ____________ in the form of ____________-flowing streams. Such streams can be dammed to form ____________ of water. The rock upon which the dam is built has to be ____________ so that the dam walls do not collapse. Water from the dam then flows rapidly down a ____________ to the ____________. There the water drives a ____________ which generates ____________. This is passed through ____________, before it is transported by ____________. Hydro-electric power is a good source of energy because it is ____________ and ____________, unlike oil or ____________.

Things to do

1. Construct a working model of a water filter. This is how you can do this:
   (a) Find a large tin (30 to 40 cm long and about 20 cm in diameter).
   (b) Punch a hole about 1 cm in diameter in the centre of the bottom of the tin.

(c) Fill the tin with stones, gravel and sand, arranged in layers as shown in the diagram below.

A model of a water filtration plant

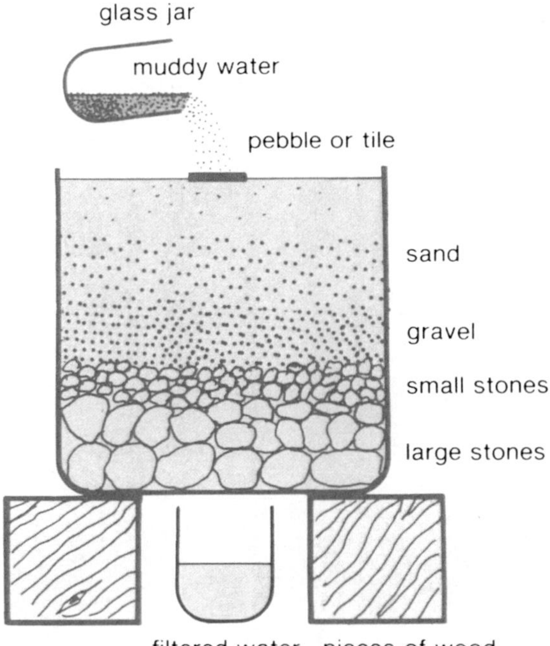

(d) Place this prepared filter on two pieces of wood or stone. Put a clean jar underneath the hole.

(e) Pour some very muddy water into the filter at the top.

(f) A pebble or tile could be used, to stop the water making a hole in the sand layer while you are pouring it in.

2. If fishing is important in your area, add some material to your scrap-book on

- how the fishing is done;
- how methods have changed in recent years;
- the main fishing areas (draw a map to show this).

You could ask a friendly fisherman for help with this information.

5. Forests and Wildlife

Forests

There are many types of forest in the world. Most of our forests are tropical forests. In such forests the top branches and leaves touch each other to form a roof, or **canopy**, above the ground. The roof of trees protects the forest soil from rain. The falling leaves and fruit help to put nutrients back into the soil. In this way the forests protect and keep the soil fertile. In turn the fertile soil helps the trees to grow. The soil needs the trees as much as the trees need the soil.

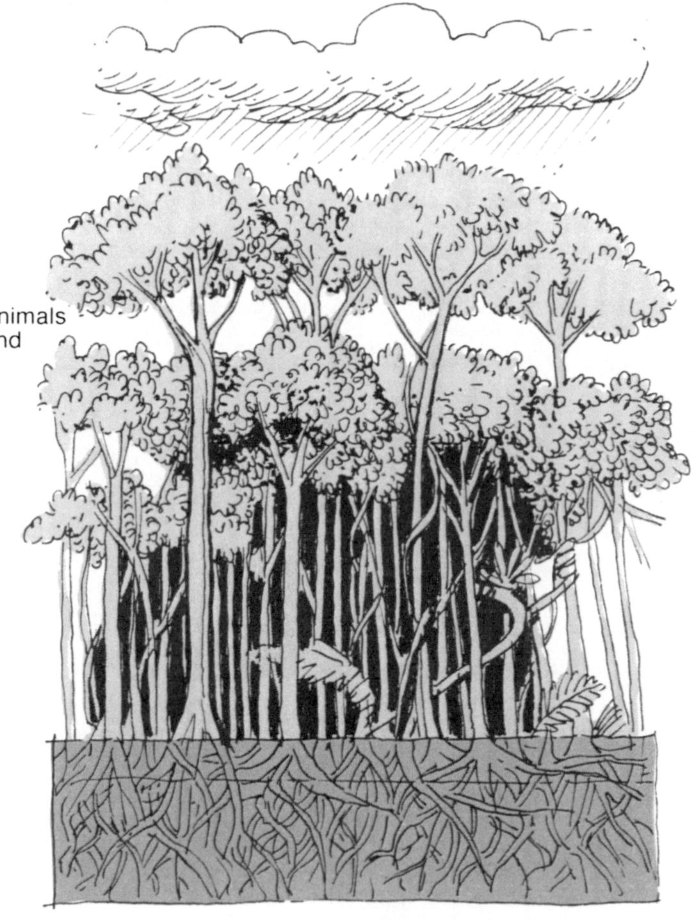

Natural rainforest.

About 87 per cent of Papua New Guinea is covered by forests, most of which are tropical forests. The remaining land is grasslands, savannah, swamp or water.

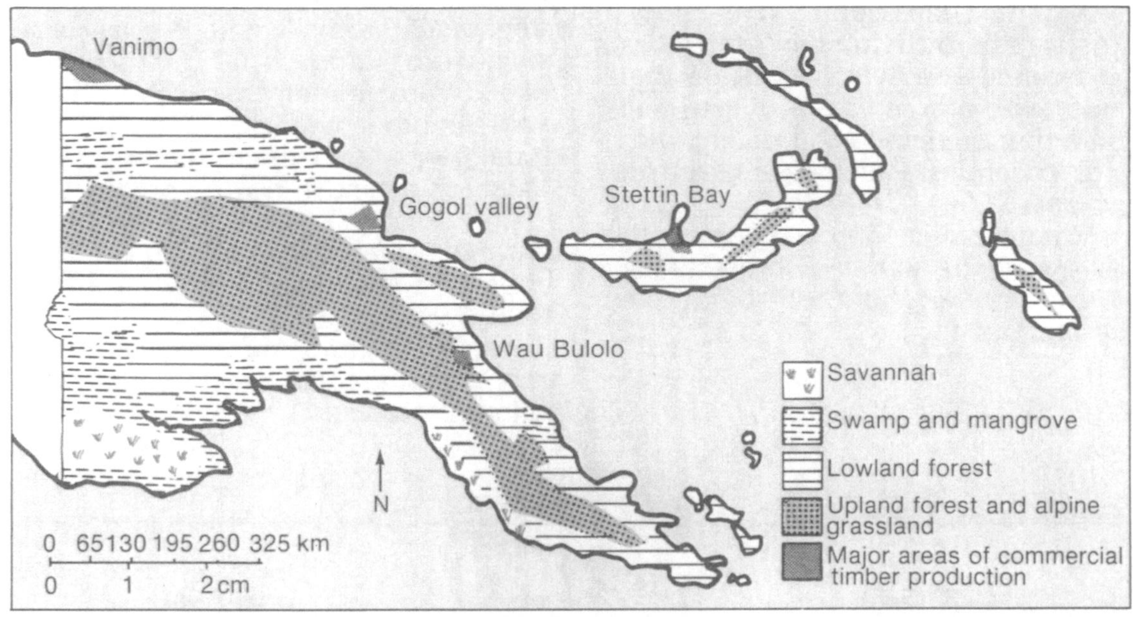

Forest resources and other vegetation in Papua New Guinea.

Tropical rainforests are part of the world's most important resources. Over half of the world's known plants grow in such forests. Many are, or could become, valuable sources of new medicines and types of food. These forests also produce most of the world's oxygen. This is the part of the air that we breathe, and without it we cannot stay alive. In the past twenty years, huge areas of the world's tropical forests have been cut down for timber or for farming. We are fortunate to have some of the world's last remaining forests. We need to be careful how we use them.

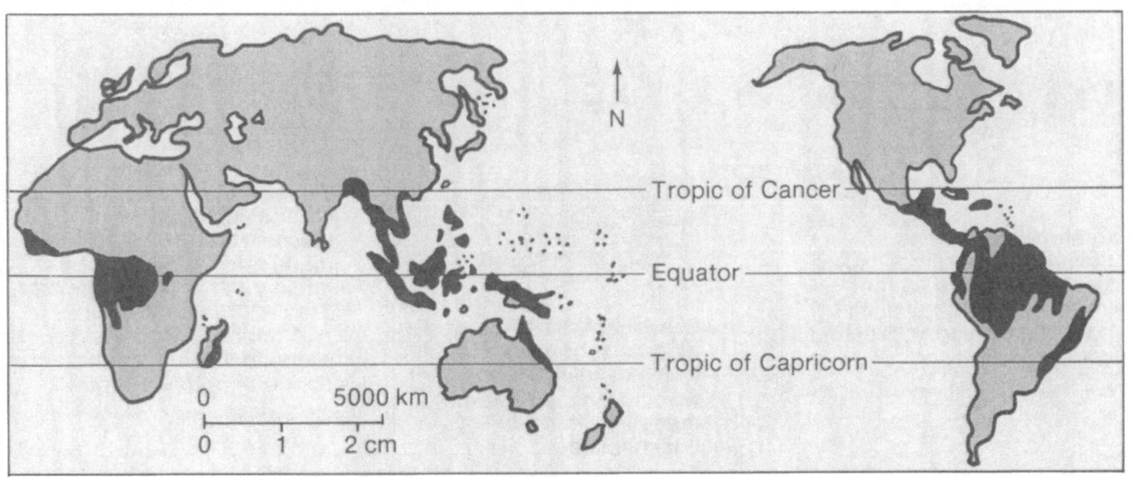

The distribution of the world's tropical rainforests.

Many thousands of different plants grow in our forests. These plants provide shelter and food for all the animals, insects and birds living in the forest. Large trees provide timber for houses and canoes. They also provide fruits, nuts, edible green leaves, medicines, firewood, materials for building, clothing, decorations, magic and religious practices.

Many of our people have a great store of knowledge about the forests they live in and have learned to use them wisely.

Timber Production

People in other countries want to buy the valuable timber which comes from trees such as rosewood, erima, kwila, walnut and taun. In 1981 more than 780 000 cubic metres of timber were sold to other countries. This earned Papua New Guinea about K45 million. Most of the timber was exported to Japan, Australia, South Korea, Taiwan and New Zealand. About 70 000 cubic metres of timber were used in Papua New Guinea.

As the diagram below shows, trees can be manufactured into a number of different products.

The trunks of large trees remain as logs or plants, and are used to make furniture and other large wooden items. Most are exported.

Some small pieces of wood are made into goods such as chopsticks, which are used in Japan and China for eating food.

Veneer: thin strips of expensive hardwoods like kwila are glued to the surface of poorer quality wood, or on to boards made of woodchips.

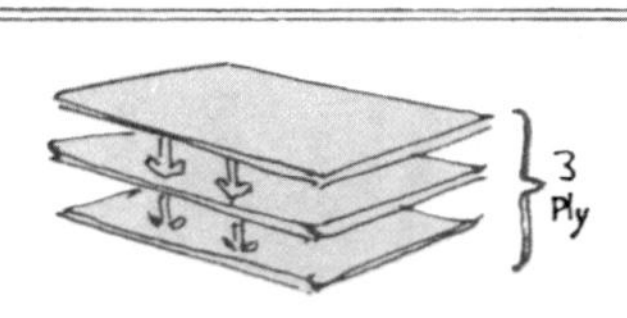

Plywood: thin strips of wood are bonded together to make thicker boards of wood. Plywood can be made in different thicknesses.

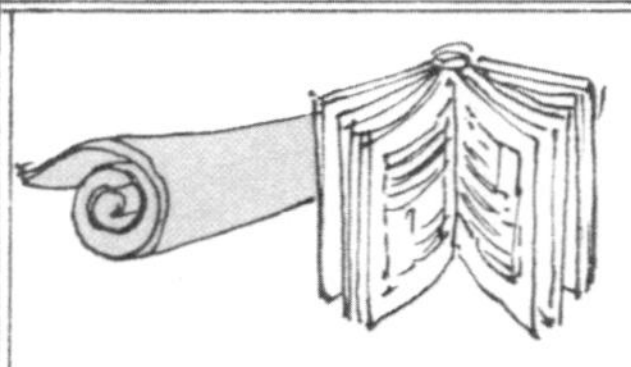

Some trees are cut into woodchips (very small pieces of wood). These are made into wood pulp by adding water and chemicals. This is then finally made into paper. The chips are produced here, but the paper is made in Japan.

Some uses of our timber.

In Papua New Guinea the people who live in nearby villages own the forests. These people are **customary land-owners**. When the government or a timber company wants to develop an area for timber production they have to make an agreement with the customary land-owners. The company is then allowed to cut the trees in the forest, but they must obey government rules to protect the environment.

In 1988 there were twenty-five timber companies in operation in Papua New Guinea. The main areas of timber production are the Bulolo valley, Lae, West New Britain, around Madang and Vanimo, parts of the Central Province and the Gulf of Papua. Some of these areas are shown on the map on page 35.

Two main methods are used to remove timber from the natural forests. They are **selective logging** and **clear felling**. In selective logging only some trees are chosen for cutting. In clear felling all the trees are cut. In selective logging young trees should be left so that they can continue to grow. Often most of the young trees are accidentally knocked over during the logging. The natural forest does not grow again. However, the government is replanting some of the area around Bulolo with native trees and trees from other countries.

Clear Felling in the Gogol Valley

A company called JANT (Japanese New Guinea Timber) is carrying out a clear-felling operation in the lowland forests of the Gogol area of Madang Province.

JANT has purchased the timber rights for twenty years from the local land-owners. All the trees of the forest are being cut down.

Most of these trees are taken to Madang. At the factory there, the trees are manufactured into woodchips. The chips are then loaded on to a ship which takes them to Japan. There they are made into cardboard and paper.

Clear felling in the Gogol valley, Madang.

A woodchip stockpile, JANT, Madang.

Large areas of the Gogol rainforest will be cut down in the next few years. There may soon be no young trees left in the Gogol area.

When the forest is cut down rain washes the soil away. There is little hope of the forest ever growing again. The government and the company are replanting some of the area with kamerere trees. These are fast-growing trees that have been introduced into Papua New Guinea.

The people of the Gogol area agreed to sell their timber. Now they find that they have lost their forest and the wildlife in it. Here is what a village man from the Gogol area said about this loss:

> I would not like my grandchildren or their grandchildren after them to be short of wildlife and to say, "Father did not think of us who were coming later. He thought only of himself, and finished off all the birds and animals, so that now I have none left."

However, as the photograph below shows, the timber companies are not the only groups responsible for damage to our forests. In some areas vegetation is burnt by our people to make hunting easier. If this burning occurs year after year, the vegetation of whole areas can change completely.

Man-made grasslands, Western Highlands Province. These grasslands are the result of burning and farming of the land.

Wildlife

There are many different types of animals in the country. They have provided our people with food, and with skins and feathers for clothing and decoration.

They are also very important in the culture of Papua New Guinea. Clans have taken animals as totems. They are an important part of the magic, ritual, myths and legends of Papua New Guinea. In some societies, animals are seen as the ancestors. Some people believe that they are the spirits of the dead, that they understand *tokples*, bring messages and tell of the change of seasons.

Many of our country's animals are not found anywhere else in the world. The Birds of Paradise are world famous. The male Raggiana Bird of Paradise is our national symbol, and appears on both the national flag and the emblem. Papua New Guinea is the home of the Alexander Birdwing, which is the world's largest butterfly. We also have the world's largest moth—the Hercules Moth. Many people visit Papua New Guinea each year to see our beautiful and rare wildlife. These animals are now a tourist resource.

In many areas there is not as much wildlife as before. The numbers of animals decrease if they are over-hunted, or if the forests they live in are destroyed. The government has now passed laws to protect fifty of our animals. These animals, called National Animals, are found only in Papua New Guinea, or are very rare.

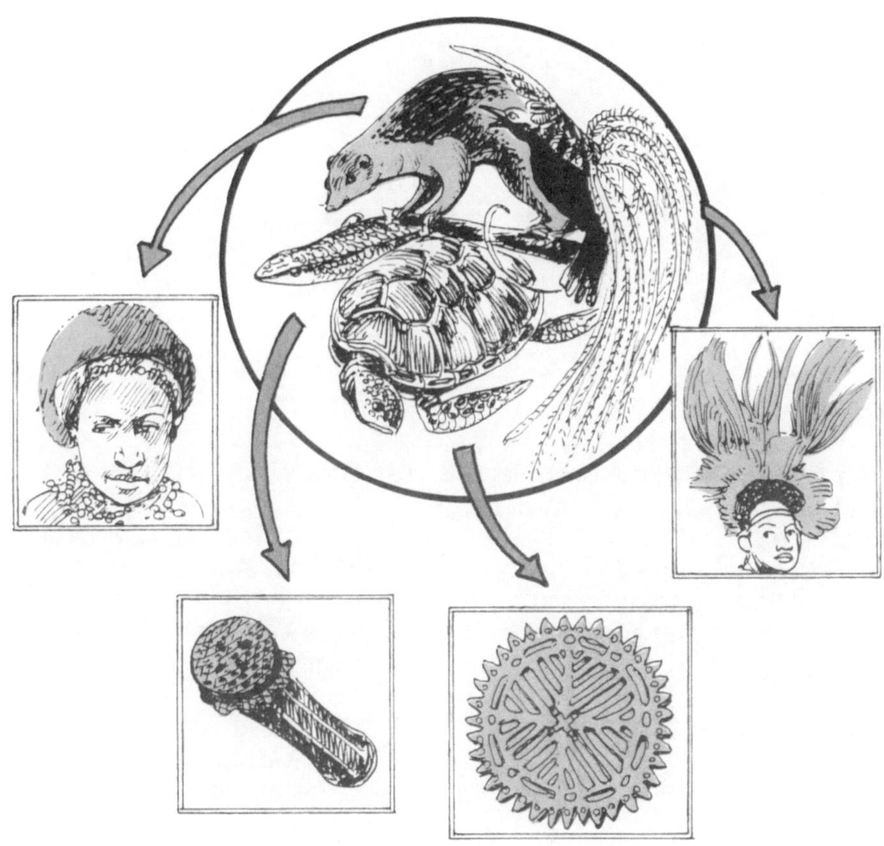

Some traditional uses of our animals.

Activities

Exercises

1. (a) Study the diagram of the forest canopy on page 34, and the diagram below. List three things which happen when the forest has been cleared.

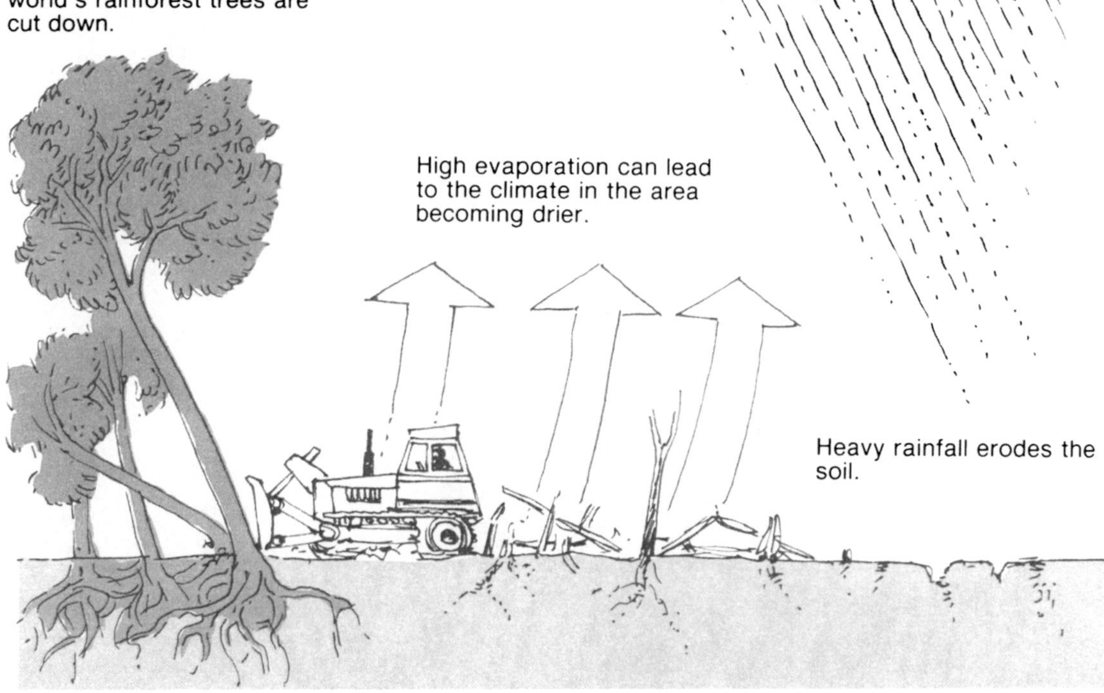

Clearing of rainforest.

(b) Make a list of the things people are likely to lose when a rainforest is cleared.

(c) What are the local people likely to gain by allowing their forest to be cleared for timber production or other uses?

2. (a) Are trees a renewable resource?

(b) Are rainforests a renewable resource?

(c) Explain the difference between the answers to (a) and (b).

3. (a) Study the map of the world's tropical forests on page 35. Using the *Papua New Guinea School Atlas*, name a country in each continent that has a large area of tropical forest.

(b) From what you have read in this chapter:

- What is happening to the size of tropical rainforests around the world?
- Compare this with what is happening to the world's deserts (chapter 4).

4. What is the difference between
   (a) chopsticks and woodchips?
   (b) veneer and plywood?
5. On a blank map of the world, mark on and name the countries to which most of our timber is exported. Join these countries to Papua New Guinea by a line showing the most likely sea route. Put an arrow on each of these lines to show the direction the timber travels.

Things to discuss

Our laws allow us to hunt protected animals with bows and arrows, but not guns. Should hunting of these animals be banned altogether?

Things to do

Continue to add information to your scrapbook. Do some research into the wildlife of your area (e.g. what types of environment do they live in? What animals are becoming rare?).

6. Minerals

Minerals are the chemical substances that together make up the Earth's rocks. Some of these minerals are valuable to man. Minerals which contain metals, like copper, gold and iron are known as **ores**.

Some rocks and minerals have always been used here. Brightly coloured minerals are often used for body decorations, and for painting religious objects. Clay is used for pottery, fire-places and decorations. Salt has always been an important mineral for adding to food. Different types of salt are found in sea water, salt water springs and in the ash of plants. The trade in salt has been important to many communities.

Stones for cooking, sago pounding and sacred objects were found in almost all places, but the special stones for making sharp, strong axes were very rare. The first mines were dug to get these stones. Stone-axe manufacture was a long and difficult process. The owners of these mines and axe factories traded these axes with many people, and became wealthy.

Gold

Some of the Europeans who first came here brought with them the knowledge and equipment for extracting metals from minerals. Iron was their most commonly used metal, but gold was their most valuable.

Gold was first discovered in this country on Sudest Island in Milne Bay Province in 1888. That year nearly 400 Australians came to the island to search for gold. Some died and many returned home sick and empty-handed. This was the beginning of modern mining in Papua New Guinea. Since then, gold has been our most valuable mineral resource.

The earliest miners found gold as tiny particles in the sands of rivers. This is called **alluvial gold**. They dug up the river beds and washed the rocks and sand to find the gold. This is called panning. Many of our people worked with these miners.

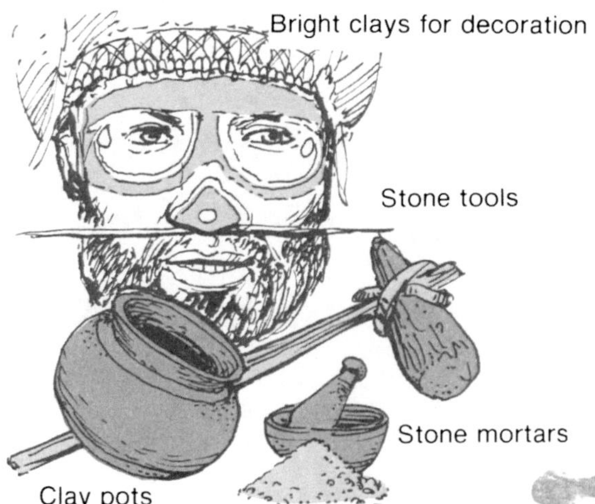

Some traditional uses of rocks and minerals.

Miners with canoe made by people from Milne Bay, 1914. (Photographer: Frank Pryke.)

After working on Sudest and other islands in Milne Bay the miners and their workers moved to the mainland to search for more gold. They followed rivers inland and they were often the first outsiders to visit many areas. At Wau and Bulolo they found great quantities of gold in the river sands. Large companies were formed, and they used huge machines, called **dredges**, to dig up the valleys and to separate out the gold. These mines closed when the Japanese invaded our country in 1942.

A gold dredge near Bulolo.

Papua New Guinean miners still mine alluvial gold along the banks of some rivers.

Gold panning near Bulolo today.

The first outsiders to visit the Highlands were Australian miners and their coastal workers looking for gold. The search for gold brought many strangers face to face. Most importantly, gold mining caused Papua New Guineans to travel and to meet their countrymen from other areas.

Mineral Exploration

Scientists know that the gold in the river beds comes from the mountains where the rivers begin. The rocks inside some of the mountains contain large quantities of gold and other valuable minerals. Searching for these deposits is called **mineral exploration**.

The National Government owns all the minerals and oil resources in Papua New Guinea. Land-owners do not own the minerals found on their land. The Department of Minerals and Energy of the National Government controls all mineral exploration work in the country. This Department gives licences to companies to look for minerals and oil. These companies spend many millions of kina each year searching for minerals.

Geologists are scientists who study rocks and how they are formed. With this knowledge they hope to be able to work out where valuable minerals can be found. They use helicopters to land at the junction of every river and stream in an area. They take samples of the rocks and sand, and send them to scientific laboratories. There, other scientists experiment on these samples to find out what minerals they contain.

In this way, geologists working in the Star Mountains in Western Province found large amounts of copper and gold in the rocks and sand of some rivers. By following these rivers upstream, they found a mountain they thought might contain copper and gold ores. This mountain was called Mount Fubilan.

Long trenches were dug across the mountains, and rock samples were taken. These samples also showed signs of valuable copper and gold. Geologists were now sure that rocks inside Mount Fubilan contained copper and gold ores. However, they did not know how much there was nor how deep it was inside the mountain. They only way to find this out was to drill deep holes into the mountain. The samples from these holes showed that there were large amounts of copper and gold ores inside Mount Fubilan.

Geologists had used similar methods to find another huge copper and gold ore deposit at Panguna in the mountains of Bougainville. At both places the government joined with overseas companies to take the valuable ore out of the ground. The companies provided the money and the technology to make this possible. Large machines were used to dig the ore out of the mountains.

The gold and copper ores were sold overseas. In return for using their money in this exploration the companies receive a large share of the profits. The National Government also earns money from its share in the mines, and from the taxes paid by the companies and their workers.

Minerals provide more than 50 per cent of our nation's export earnings. The mines employ thousands of people. Many other people are employed to provide shipping, **accounting**, building, **legal** and other services for the mines.

Mt Fubilan.

Panguna—A Case Study

The open-cut mine Bougainville Copper Limited. (Reprinted with kind permission of Bougainville Copper Limited.)

Construction of the mine began in the late 1960s. A road was built from the coast to the mine site in the mountains. At the mine a new town, called Panguna, was built for the mine workers and their families, who came from all parts of the world.

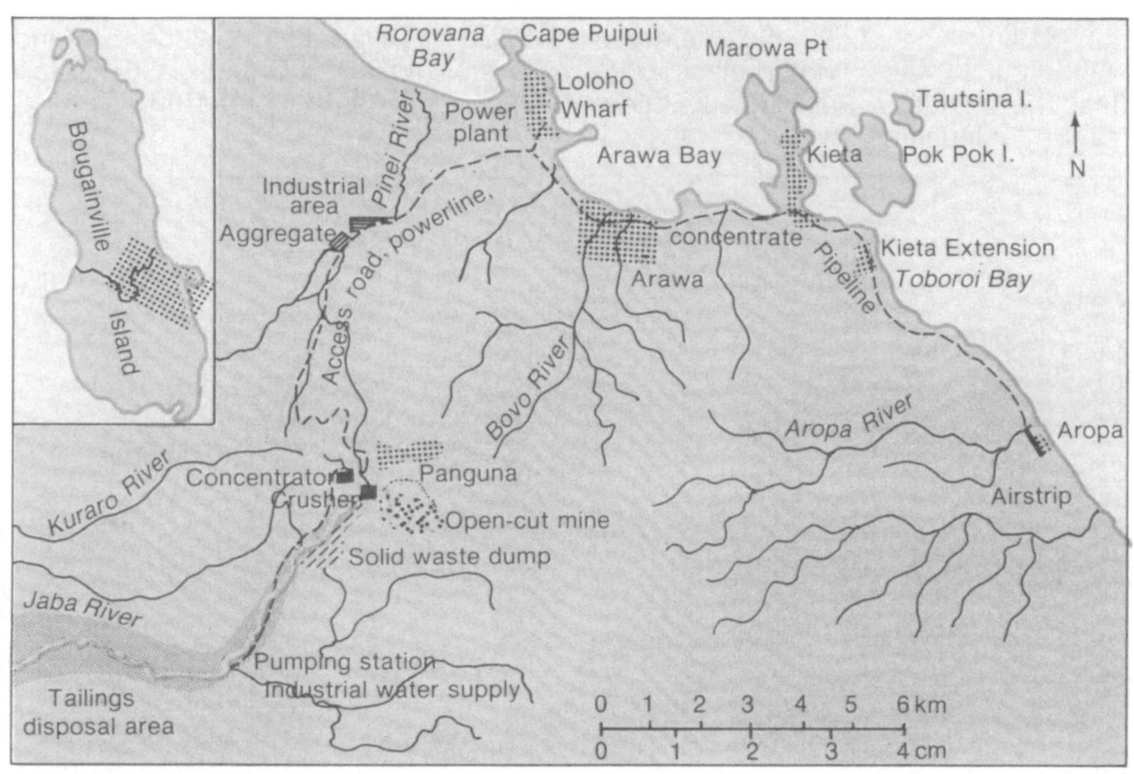

The copper mine at Panguna.

The mine is one of the biggest of its kind in the world. Large machines and explosives are used to dig the ore out of the ground. The mountain has now gone. There is a large hole where it used to be. A factory was also built to crush the ore and to separate the valuable minerals from the waste rock. What is left is called **copper concentrate**. It is then mixed with water and sent down a pipeline to Loloho, a new port on the coast. From here it is exported by ship, mostly to Japan and West Germany.

The mine has brought many benefits to the people of Papua New Guinea and Bougainville. Money is paid to the North Solomons Provincial Government. Land owners have received compensation for damage done to their land. Many people in the province are employed by the mine. They receive training in many kinds of work at the mine. The province is one of the richest and most developed.

However, the mine has also brought some problems. One problem is the effect of the mine on the environment. More than 50 million tonnes of waste rock are poured each year into the Jaba River near the mine. This has killed fish by poisoning the water, and it has also spoiled large areas of land. Father John Momis, a leader of the Bougainville people, has expressed many concerns on the effects of the mine on his people and their land. He feels that the people of his island will be left with "pollution and a giant hole where once there was a mountain". Father Momis also argues that the people of Papua New Guinea need "companies that do not grow uncontrollably, but follow Melanesian traditions, which return profits to the people". He feels that the company has "employed some of our finest men, who have ceased serving their people, and instead serve the company". Another problem is that there are fewer people willing or available to work the land. This will cause problems in the future when the mine is **exhausted**.

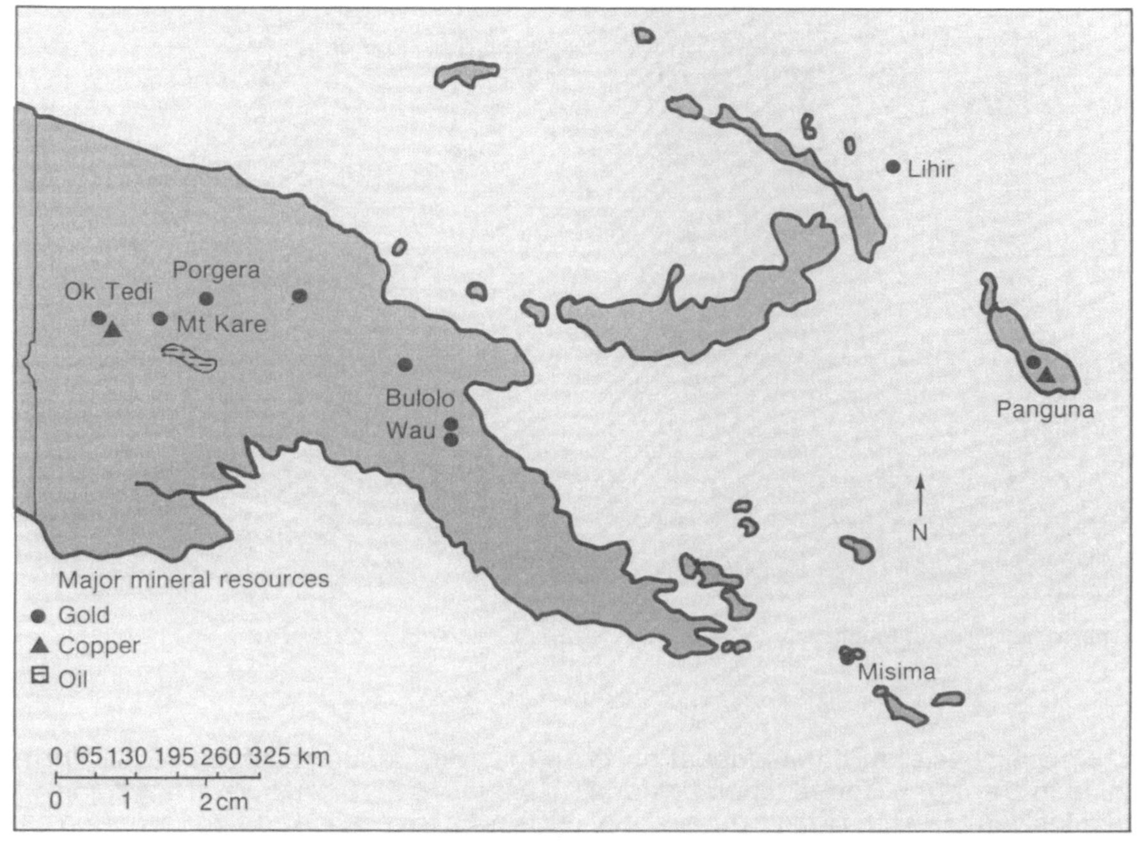

Major mining and prospecting areas of Papua New Guinea.

Other Mining Projects

Many other deposits of minerals and oil have been found in Papua New Guinea. The map above shows the location of some of these mineral and oil resources. The gold mine on Misima Island in the Milne Bay Province opened recently. Plans are under way to build gold mines at Porgera in the Enga Province, Lihir Island in the New Ireland Province and for the production of oil in the Southern Highlands Province. The National Government, Provincial Governments, the companies and the people, all know the benefits and potential problems of such projects. The planners hope to avoid as many of the problems as possible.

The World

Important minerals and oil are found in many different countries of the world. The USSR is the largest producer of most metals. Australia, the United States of America and South Africa are also major producers. Most of the world's oil comes from the USA, the USSR, Indonesia and Venezuela, and from countries in the Middle East and North Africa.

Mineral **reserves** are areas of minerals that we know about but have not yet mined. The map below shows where some of the world's most important reserves are.

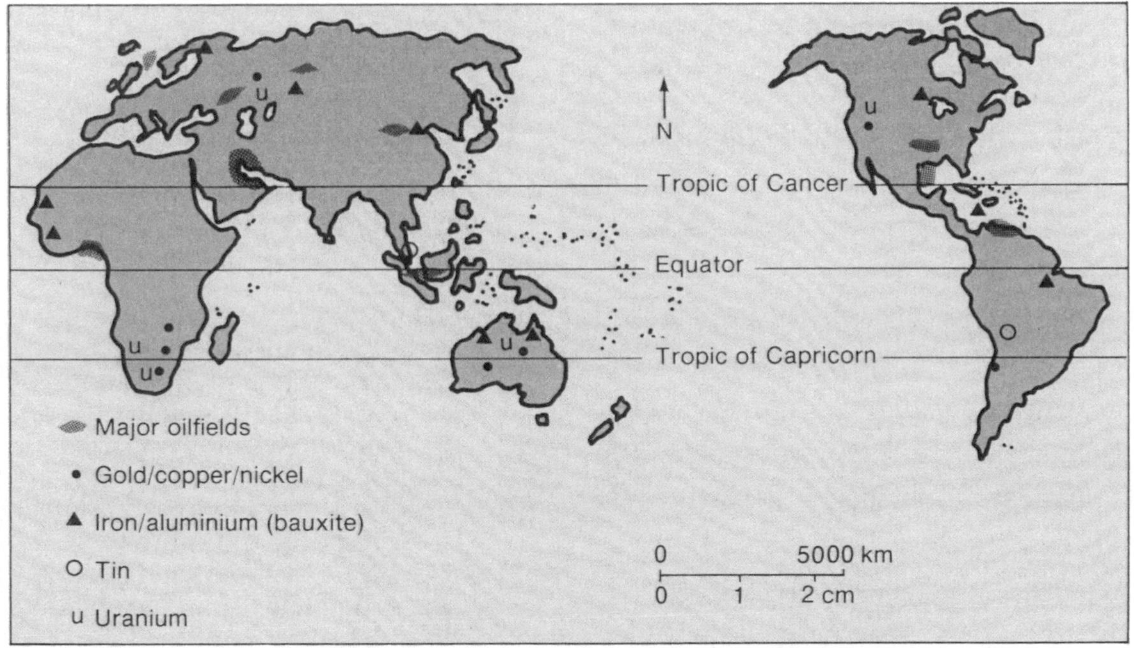

The location of some of the world's major mining areas.

Activities

Exercises

1. **(a)** Explain, in sentences, what rocks, minerals and ores are.
(b) List four traditional uses of rocks and minerals in your area.

2. From the words in the list below fill in the blanks:

alluvial, Sudest, Wau, explorers, river, panning, Bulolo, changes, dredges, 1888.

Gold was first found in Papua New Guinea on __________ Island in __________. Most of the early gold was found in __________ deposits. This gold is called __________ gold. At first this gold was obtained by __________, but later __________ were used. The largest goldfields were at __________ and __________. The early miners were important __________ of our country in their search for gold. They brought great __________ to the people in many of the areas where they mined.

3. The search for a gold mountain:

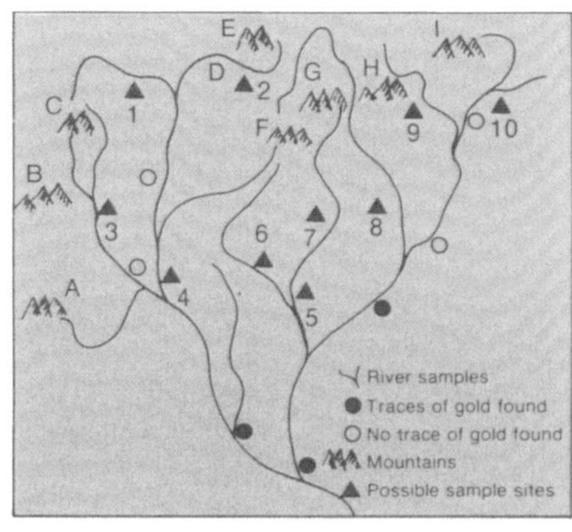

Find the gold mountain.

Imagine you are a geologist working in the area shown on the map above. You have found traces of gold at three of the seven sites shown on the map.

(a) Of the possible sites, marked 1 to 10 on the map, which would be the next five you would choose?
(b) Which of the mountains, marked A to I, do you think is the "gold mountain"?
(c) Describe what you would do next to prove that you are right.

4. Study the map of the site of the Bougainville Copper Mine on page 47.

(a) How far is it from the mine to the coast?
(b) What two processing plants are found near the mine?
(c) Explain simply, in a sentence or two, what these do with the copper ore, and why they do it (clues: waste, pipeline).
(d) Where is the wharf from which the copper is exported?
(e) How long is the copper concentrate pipeline from the mine to the wharf?
(f) From the map, draw a flow diagram to show what happens to the copper as it goes from the mine to the wharf.
(g) What two signs of damage to the environment are shown on the map?
(h) Panguna is an open-cast mine. What do you think this term means? (The photograph of the mine on page 46 should help you.)

5. Using the map on page 48 and the *Papua New Guinea School Atlas*, copy and complete the following:

(a) __________ is an island near New Ireland where gold has been found.

(b) ____________ is an island in Milne Bay where gold has been found.

(c) ____________ is a gold site in Enga Province.

(d) ____________ is a large copper and gold mine in Western Province.

(e) ____________ is a province in which there is much oil exploration.

6. Using the map on page 49 and the *Papua New Guinea School Atlas*:

(a) Name three countries where oil mining is important.

(b) Name three countries with large deposits of iron and aluminium ores.

(c) Name three countries, besides Papua New Guinea, where gold and copper mining is important.

(d) Which country in South-east Asia is a major producer of tin?

Things to discuss

Discuss the advantages and disadvantages of mining:

(a) for the people of the area involved,

(b) for the country as a whole.

Things to do

Put in your scrapbook any newspaper cuttings about mining that you can find. Write your own comment for each one. If you live in an area where mining is important, write a short paragraph describing how the mining there is changing people's lives.

7. Human Resources

People and Tradition

People are a country's most important resource Our skills, knowledge and respect for the land on which we live has enabled us to live and develop it over many thousands of years. These things are part of our traditions.

Children are taught these things by their families. All children learn the spiritual and moral values of their clan. Boys are taught skills such as hunting, fishing and house building. Girls are taught cooking, gardening, crafts and child care. Selected children are taught the magic, medicine and land rights of the clan.

A kundu-maker passes on his skills.

Population

There are more than 3 million people living in Papua New Guinea. The government tries to provide services such as health care, education, agricultural assistance, and security for all our people. Many of us have large families. Because of improved health care fewer people die young. This means that the number of people here is growing rapidly.

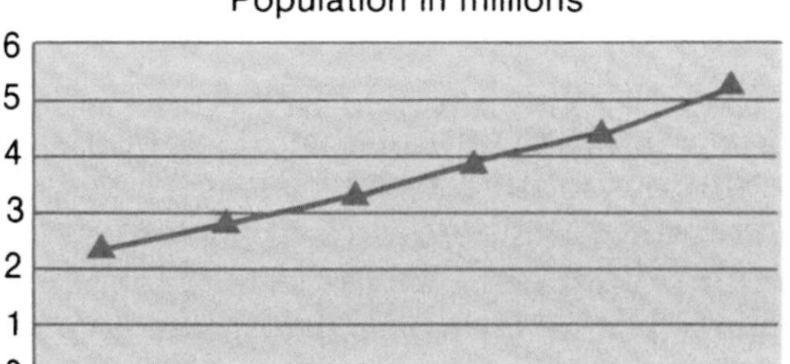

Population growth in Papua New Guinea.

If a larger population means we can grow more crops and build more roads then that is good. If, on the other hand, it means that more people use the country's services but do not produce anything, then it is a problem.

Health

Healthy people work better than sick people. The government is trying very hard to bring health services, better food and clean water to all our people. Our standards of health are improving, but there are still a number of health problems. These include diseases such as malaria, diarrhoea, tuberculosis and malnutrition. Some of these diseases can kill.

We can measure how healthy we are compared with other countries. One way of doing this is by finding the average age at which people die. This is called a country's **life expectancy**. Another way is to find out how many children die in the country. **Infant death rates** show how many children die, out of every thousand born, before they reach the age of one. The table below shows life expectancies and infant death rates for several countries.

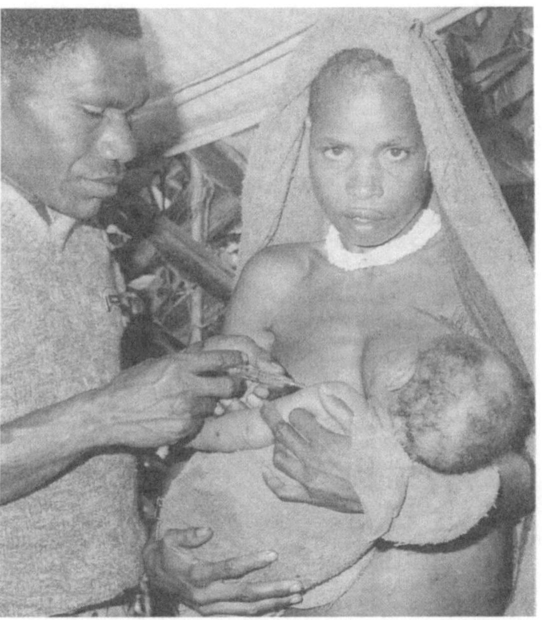

Health care for a Chimbu child.

Country	Life expectancy	Deaths of babies under 1(/1000 born)
P.N.G.	53	69
Guinea (in Africa)	39	176
China	69	36
Japan	78	6
Australia	76	9

Look at the differences between the countries. Why do you think 176 out of every 1000 babies in Guinea die before the age of 1, yet only 6 out of every 1000 Japanese babies die during the same period?
Find the countries mentioned on a world map.

Life expectancy and infant death rates.

Education

When people discuss "education" in Papua New Guinea today they talk about the number of people at school and the subjects they study. This could make people think that we are a country of ignorant and uneducated people. In fact there has always been a strong system of traditional education for all our people.

The Western education system is new to Papua New Guinea. Missionaries who accompanied the first European colonists started this new system of education. They built schools to introduce us to Christian beliefs and principles and to provide us with skills needed to support their work.

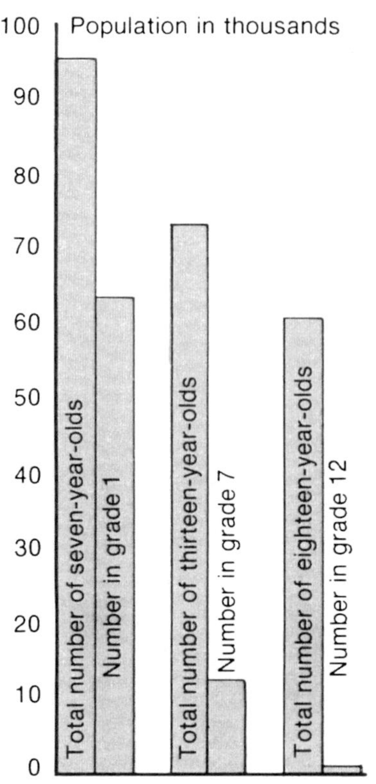

The share of the population receiving schooling.

In the 1950s the colonial government built schools to train selected people to work in their administration. Since then attendance at school and the gaining of paid employment has been seen as proof that you were successfully "educated". This Western type of education grew rapidly in the 1960s and 1970s. Many of the graduates of this system are contributing to our development as doctors, engineers, teachers and other paid workers.

Recently the Government has realised the danger of our schools ignoring our traditional system of education. We are having to think again about why we are sending our children to school. **Paid employment can no longer be the main reason**. There are simply not enough paid jobs for everybody. Many Grade 6 and Grade 10 graduates are returning to their communities where there is, and always has been, traditional work for them. Some graduates, however, no longer value village life and traditions, and choose to come to towns. They find no work in the towns and often join gangs and become criminals.

In 1986 the Government wrote a book called *A Philosophy of Education for Papua New Guinea*. This book talks about the need for schools to bring together the traditional and Western systems of education. The Government does not want our schools to continue to produce people just for paid employment. It wants students who respect their traditions and will live happily in their villages, who can earn their own living, who like and respect each other, and who will willingly work together for the benefit of their families, communities and country.

The Government wants to do this by encouraging *tokples* pre-schools, by teaching traditional values, agriculture, arts and crafts and by involving the home, the church and the community in the education of children.

Activities

Exercises

1. **(a)** Why do you think that in the past most Papua New Guineans wanted many children?
   (b) Explain in your own words what is meant by "More people means that we have more resources, but we also use more resources".
   (c) Study the graph on page 53. What was (or will be) Papua New Guinea's total population in each of these years:
   1971? 1986? 1996?
2. Study the graph on page 54, then answer the following:

   Number of 7-year-old children in the country?

   Number in Grade 1?
   Fraction of 7-year-old children in Grade 1?

   Number of 13-year-old children in the country?
   Number in Grade 7?
   Fraction of 13-year-old children in Grade 7?

   Number of 18-year-old people in the country?
   Number in Grade 12?
   Fraction of 18-year-old people in Grade 12?
3. **(a)** Ten people died this year in an imaginary country. The ages they died at are shown below. What is the life expectancy in this country?

   17, 72, 45, 56, 57, 51, 83, 1, 37, 63.

   (b) Using the information in the table on page 53, draw bar graphs to show the average life expectancy in Papua New Guinea, Guinea (in Africa) and Australia.
   (c) Papua New Guinea's environment is, and its life expectancy used to be, similar to that found in Guinea. What has happened to our life expectancy over the last fifty years. Why has this happened?
   (d) Give three reasons why Australians, on average, live longer than Papua New Guineans.

Things to discuss

1. "Papua New Guinea should try to increase its population as fast as it can." Do you agree?
2. Read the two extracts below, and then answer the questions that follow.

> I grew to be one of the leaders, and if we said "let's go and work in the food gardens", everyone went and nobody played the bighead.
>
> But now, all the educated ones don't have any regard for our authority—they all want to be boss. They don't know about garden work. Rice and tin fish from the store is all they want to know about. The ways of our ancestors carried authority and respect, but they are going.
>
> My father-in-law taught me the rain magic. He gave me power over both sun and the rain. If I had a child who would listen I would pass the magic on to him.
>
> Siasu Martin, rainmaker,
> New Ireland
>
> The old customs are dying out, but that doesn't worry me. I am not passing on our old customs to my children. Instead I want them to receive a modern education. One of my children works with the Agriculture Department, one with the Commerce Department, one is at University and two are still at school.
>
> John Tone, farmer, West Sepik

(a) • What is Siasu Martin's opinion on how valuable traditions are?
- Why do you think he thinks this way?

(b) • What are John Tonte's opinions of this?
- Why do you think he thinks this way?

(c) In small groups discuss, and make a list, of all the things in your culture
- that should be preserved,
- that should not be preserved.

8. Conservation

In this book we have looked at how people use their skills and knowledge in their environment. We have studied the relationships between human and natural resources.

The traditional methods of using resources and the modern methods are very different.

In the traditional ways we use our resources in small amounts. We use them to provide for our own needs and the needs of our near-neighbours. Modern development, however, uses as much of a resource as possible. In the past our ancestors chipped off pieces of rock to make axe blades. Today we remove mountains to find the minerals they contain.

Conservation of resources means using them wisely.

Conservation has always been important in our traditional life. We have developed ways of looking after our soils. We have controlled hunting and fishing to allow wildlife to breed and multiply. We have protected forest areas and water sources. These practices have protected our resources for thousands of years.

By conserving our resources, we produce goods, satisfy our needs and improve our standard of living. At the same time, we keep resources for the future.

We have only recently begun to use our resources in the modern way. This means that we still have most of our natural resources. They are available for our use today and for the use of future generations. It also means that our natural environment is still mostly undamaged.

In the modern world, we use resources much faster. We now have the power to make great changes and do serious damage to our environment. Clear felling of forests, such as that in the Gogol area, for example, causes permanent loss of our forests.

Over-fishing is another serious danger. The example of crayfish harvesting in the Central Province shows what can happen. Crayfish breed in the reefs off Yule Island. Each year the people caught many thousands. They sold them overseas for high prices. Recently a Japanese fishing company bought the rights to catch crayfish. They used large boats with **electronic** equipment to follow the crayfish. They trapped huge numbers. Within two years the numbers dropped dramatically. The boats then went away. Today the village people can catch only small amounts. The crayfish resource has been badly damaged.

Modern weapons, like guns, have also reduced the numbers of wildlife. More people hunting with better weapons can cause some species of wildlife to become extinct. The dugong is one example of an animal in danger of extinction. The dugong is a sea mammal which eats sea-grasses in shallow waters. Until 1960 there were plenty of dugongs along the coast of Central Province. The use of guns and motor boats has made it much easier to catch dugongs. As a result they are rarely seen today.

Pollution of our environment now is another serious problem. Pollution takes place in many ways. Waste from mines or factories can poison the rivers and seas. The waste gases from factories and motor vehicles pollute the air.

In Papua New Guinea we can learn from the mistakes of other countries. The government has made some laws to protect our environment and many of our animals. Only traditional weapons are allowed for hunting creatures such as Birds of Paradise. There are other laws to protect our fish from foreign fishing fleets.

There are National Parks and Wildlife Management Areas. They conserve our forests and animals.

The government also tries to control the activities of mining and logging companies.

All our own people must participate in the protection of our environment. We must combine modern science and the traditional conservation practices and knowledge. Modern technical knowledge has caused some people to lose confidence in their traditional ways. The traditional ways are important in the protection, conservation and development of our valuable resources.

Pollution caused by motor vehicles.

Activities

Things to do

Conservation is not just about reading things in books and doing exercises in the classroom. It is about the way **all of us** approach our environment. If we are careless with our environment this will destroy it. Caring is not enough though. People need to do something positive. *You* can help in two ways:

1. Do something practical. Is there a small project your class could undertake? Could you clean up a local stream? Or help to replant a small area of forest?
2. Educate others. Encourage people who live near the school to come and see your scrapbook displays. Talk to them, and explain some of the things you have learnt. In this way perhaps you can help others to be concerned about preserving our environment. (After all, it does not matter how much you care for our forests if somebody else burns them down. The end result is the same!)

Glossary

Word	Page	Meaning
accounting services	45	The keeping of financial or money records for a company.
colonized	18	One country takes over control of another and sometimes people from the first country migrate to the second.
conservation	57	Looking after and protecting the natural environment from wasteful use.
customary land-owners	37	A group of people who traditionally own the land around a village but without written proof.
deposits	48	Rocks containing mineral wealth, such as gold, oil or copper.
electronic	57	Equipment using very small electrical devices, such as computers and televisions.
erosion	17	The washing away of soil by heavy rain.
exhausted	48	When all the minerals in a mine have been finished or used up.
fertile	16	Containing many different elements to produce good crops.
filtered	27	Water passed through sand so that material in the water is trapped between the sand grains.
irrigation	27	Adding water to crops artificially.
legal services	45	Advice on matters to do with the law.
nucleus estate	19	A central plantation surrounded by many small-holders who provide extra crops.
nutrients	14	The parts of a soil that are essential for healthy plant growth.
outgrowers	19	Farmers with small farms who produce crops for plantation on a nucleus estate.
pollution	57	The poisoning or spoiling of the environment.
reservoirs	26	Lakes made by the building of dams across rivers.
self-sufficient	8	Producing all your needs yourself.
specialize	8	Concentrate on making or doing one thing so that you become better at it.
technology	1	Ways of using resources to make other things.

Index